EVANGELICAL PERSPECTIVES

Toward a Biblical Balance

Dr. Ronald B. Mayers

Professor of Philosophy and Religion
Grand Rapids Baptist College

UNIVERSITY
PRESS OF
AMERICA

LANHAM • NEW YORK • LONDON

Copyright © 1987 by

University Press of America,® Inc.

4720 Boston Way
Lanham, MD 20706

3 Henrietta Street
London WC2E 8LU England

British Cataloging in Publication Information Available

Scripture quotations are from the New American Standard Bible,
Copyright © The Lockman Foundation
1960, 1962, 1963, 1968, 1971, 1972, 1973, 1975, 1977.

Library of Congress Cataloging in Publication Data
Mayers, Ronald B.
    Evangelical perspectives.

    Bibliography: p.
        1. Evangelicalism.   2. Theology, Doctrinal.
I. Title.
BR1640.M39   1987   230'.044   86-28966
ISBN 0-8191-6062-8 (alk. paper)
ISBN 0-8191-6063-6 (pbk. : alk. paper)

All University Press of America books are produced on acid-free
paper which exceeds the minimum standards set by the National
Historical Publication and Records Commission.

DEDICATION

Prayerfully, our children, Stephen and Charissa, have
been raised in the framework of the Christian teaching
and attitude that is expressed here. May they, and I,
as well as my past and future students, be disciples of
balanced doctrine that is truly biblical.

iii

ACKNOWLEDGMENTS

A special "thank you" to my past theology teachers: Drs. Keller, Lightner and Thomas of Baptist Bible Seminary; Drs. Osterhaven and Oudersluys of Western Theological Seminary; and Drs. Jamison, Hall, Robertson, and Vahanian of Syracuse University. In a less academic, but very practical manner, may I also express my appreciation of Mrs. Debbie Katip who typed the manuscript for this UPA publication.

TABLE OF CONTENTS

PREFACE

The early church battle concerning the Person of Christ lasted for some three hundred years, ending with the biblical perspective that Jesus was both totally divine and completely human. This example of biblical balance is the same doctrinal maturity that is needed today. For instance, contemporary debate in regard to the process of Scriptural inspiration must similarly conclude that the Bible was neither dropped from heaven like a rock, nor is it the product of human ingenuity, but is the unique production of God's Spirit and man's pen.

These two doctrines illustrate the need for biblical balance that is the goal and purpose of this book. Building on the historic orthodox perspective of both God and creation, the trinity as both one and many, and Jesus Christ as both distinctively human and totally divine, the remaining chapters demonstrate that an identical balance is needed in many of the doctrines that divide conservative Christians if a truly encompassing biblicism, the proclaimed goal of both sides of such debates, is to be attained.

CHAPTER I

NECESSITY OF DOCTRINAL BALANCE

Doctrinal balance! What is it? Why is it necessary? How come it has been so elusive throughout the history of the Christian church?

Questions such as these, and hopefully answers, are the purpose of this book. Christians of all perspectives and persuasions have had trouble finding balance in the many nuances of doctrine, worship, and practice as is perhaps evident in the proliferation of denominational outlooks.

This work is not an attempt at ecumenical theology that ventures to cross all bridges of differences by some eclectic fashion that leaves no one satisfied and all more determined to maintain their peculiar differences, be they doctrinal, governmental, or practical. Rather it is intended for conservative Christians of various denominational stances to see the doctrinal balance that the Bible seems to imply for so many of the theological issues that have historically divided us. Many of our seminaries advertise this balance, but when the student enters the theological or apologetic classroom, balance on many issues continues to elude both the professor and his students. Even the one doctrine that defines Christianity per se, the person of Christ, seems to defy a biblical understanding of both his absolute godness as well as his humanness. But this is the Scriptural teaching. But how do we express it without either to some extent denying his deity to assert his true humanity, or vice versa. The ancient church had this as its first theological issue. Pastors and theologians of note struggled to state the doctrine--Arius, Nestorius, Sabellius, and Athanasius who history has given the label of orthodoxy, that is, established doctrine.

It is the contention of this book that established doctrine, or orthodoxy, has usually been, and should always be, determined by the balance that the Bible indicates in the various doctrinal issues that the church must explain and elucidate to her members. This has not always been the case in American evangelicalism and fundamentalism. Many "bible believing" denominations exist, not because of governmental differences of polity, but over a slightly different understanding of man, sin, salvation--be it its inception or its

1

continuance. Similarly, in the past decade evangelicals and fundamentalists have divided over the very
foundation of their beliefs--THE BIBLE!!! Like the
issue in regard to Jesus Christ, the question now is
debated as to whether the Bible can be the Word of God
while at the same time it is the word of man. Deep
hurts are on both sides. The division appears needless
if both sides would reckon with the balance of historic
orthodoxy in regard to the Scriptures themselves.

There are areas of division other than the purely
doctrinal or theological. The way in which we worship
is very different across the various conservative
denominations. There is the constant debate of form
versus freedom. Neither perspective totally excludes
the other. That is, there is always some structure or
form even to the worship service that is perceived as
unstructured, free or random. Likewise, the most
liturgical service provides freedom to express oneself
differently or to slightly change the order of service.
There is no need to have one common worship service
across denominational emphases, though Baptists are to
some degree becoming more formal, while the Episcopal
church is opening its doors to renewal which includes a
more free participation by the laity in the midst of
worship. It is this balance of form and freedom that
seems to be emerging in our attitudes to worship that
is being asked of us also in areas of doctrinal
divergence. Is there any common ground on those issues
that encompass the controversy surrounding the Scriptures themselves, or the way in which we understand the
mission of the Church, that allow us to attain the same
balance that seemingly is happening in regard to
worship?

There are also questions of methodology that
underlie many of these doctrinal misunderstandings.
The primary question is the question of starting point.
By this we mean, do we begin all theological pursuits
by beginning with God, or are there avenues of attention in which we as men must begin with ourselves?
This question of method is most clearly seen in the
understanding of salvation. Is there any way in which
man is responsible to respond to the grace of God, or
is God's grace absolutely irresistible? This is at the
heart of the dispute between Arminians and Calvinists
across all evangelical and fundamentalist lines.
Similarly, the century long debate in the area of
Christian apologetics flounders on this issue of
methodology. Those labeled presuppositionalists,

2

usually always Calvinists theologically, insist that man can never end with God if he doesn't intellectually begin with God as one's basic assumption. The so-called evidentialists, frequently more Arminian in theology, argue that man made in God's image must interpret the revelational evidence that God gives to his reality and saving work to truly know God. The debate is really only the methodological issue of the a priori versus the a posteriori so prominent in the history of philosophy, now appearing in Christian dress.[1]

Either of the above "objectivist" methodologies would be highly suspect to those Christians who stress, and rightly, that Christianity is a personal experience. For these Christians the objective criteria of either apologetic method is really irrelevant. Soren Kierkegaard complained bitterly nearly 150 years ago of the cold objectivity of so much of Christian life and practice. He rightly argued that Christian faith is more than just an affirmation of correct doctrine or historical evidence of its truthfulness. At the same time many Kierkegaardian followers have dismissed the objective, be it a priori or a posteriori for what Kierkegaard himself may have labeled a leap of faith. True Christian faith is a way of life, a whole manner of being, but the emphasis on the personal or "subjective" does not eliminate the questions of philosophic method, or of historical objectivity and evidence of the incarnation of Jesus, the Christ. Both the objective and subjective must be balanced in any issue, be it intellectual or practical. This necessary balance that is coming to the fore in Christian apologetics and philosophy is also needed in those on-going areas of doctrinal disagreements.

Church history shows us this balance in various doctrinal debates of previous generations. The most obvious is the Christological and trinitarian debates of the third and fourth centuries. Church history also shows us expressions of extreme in doctrinal and practical areas of church life. One such area was the great difference of what it meant to live a Christian life. Was one to be an ascetic and live a life that is self-denying to the extreme of even being life-threatening? Was one to withdraw to the desert and live as a hermit, which some did? Or was the monastic way of life sufficiently self-denying without going to the previous extremes? Though for many, the monastic life removed individuals from the world in which Christ seemingly sent His disciples and thus prohibited them from really being the "salt of the earth and the light of the world." What was one to do? H. Richard Niebuhr's classic work enumerates the major perspectives that Christian communities and traditions took in attempting to solve this Christ and culture dilemma.[2]

There are thus numerous issues which have divided members of Christendom throughout her history. A present non-doctrinal issue that divides the evangelical world are political perspectives between the evangelical left represented by such publications as the Sojourners periodical, and the New Right which in the general public eyes is most frequently thought of as the Moral Majority. Both of these particular organizations are caring as evidenced by the Sojourners community in Washington, D.C., or the numerous homes for unwed mothers as an alternative to abortion that are supported by those closely associated with Moral Majority. The easy polarity of love on the left and hate, or at least intolerance, on the right is simply a very poor conceptualization. This is not to say there are not real political differences between the evangelical left and right. If one were to discuss armaments, for instance, there would be very little agreement. Conventional arms would fare little better than nuclear when discussing the proportion of monies for budgetary purposes versus domestic social needs by those of the political left. There would be no balanced position seemingly possible when one side advocates total nuclear disarmament, even perhaps unilaterally, if the other perspective apparently supports even the present "star-wars" scenario. Similarly, positions of self-defense and absolute pacificism do not present much room for a compromise posture. Certainly, the political debate over the defense budget by conservative Christians usually has this facet of doctrinal disagreement in regard to war, or one's involvement in it, as a philosophic factor in one's political ideology. Not all political disagreements are as philosophic or theologically rooted. Political perspectives frequently differ due to one's sociological status within a society. It is no different with evangelical and fundamentalist Christians. A bigger picture needs to be painted for both sides. A picture hopefully colored with strokes of biblical brushings that indicate the inherent worth of every individual, rich or poor, blue or white collar, with distinctive etchings of social justice for all, much like Amos sought for ancient Israel. The biblical demand for

4

justice would seem to be a place that the political spectrums within conservative Christianity might begin to find a balanced setting to pursue one's Christian calling.

The purpose of this introductory chapter is not, however, to attempt to solve the many issues where a balanced outlook is so desperately needed. Our purpose here is simply to demonstrate that there are so many avenues in which the Christian church is involved that do cry out for the need of a stance of tolerance and equilibrium. Our concerns, however, are not political, though some might interpret chapter 12 regarding the task of the church in such light. Rather our concerns are really academic and doctrinal for the Christian college student as well as the parish clergy and laymen who desire a more balanced perspective to the theological issues that continue to divide much of the conservative Protestant world. It is hoped that the doctrinal positions taken on issues that we debate might not be simply adopted, but might cast a frame of mind that is open for nuances of truth that so often escape us in our own particular corners of Christendom. Might we find an orthodox stance on these current topics much as the ancient church did in regard to the person of Christ and His necessary place in the trinitarian Godhead.

REFLECTION

1. What is the purpose of this book? How is the purpose related to the history of doctrine within the Christian church?

2. For whom is this book written? Why? Is this a worthwhile task?

3. Discuss a few of the areas in which a greater balance is needed or being achieved in the church that are other than doctrinal issues.

4. What are methodological issues? How do they underlie most doctrinal disagreements. Is a balanced position impossible in these issues? Defend your answer to the previous question.

[1]See Ronald B. Mayers, <u>Both/And: A Balanced Apologetic</u> (Chicago: Moody Press, 1984).

[2]See H. Richard Niebuhr, <u>Christ and Culture</u> (New York: Harper & Row, 1951).

CHAPTER II

REALITY: BOTH GOD AND CREATION

Reality--what is it? This question, along with its partner--what is truth?--has been asked for millennia. Ancient Greek philosophers identified water or air as the final or ultimate reality. As one searches for the answer to this question, another appears. Is reality permanent? Surely whatever is "really" real does not change! How could it and be the really real? And still, what is there that doesn't change? Everything we know, including ourselves, changes. Is there nothing permanent?

Nearly all philosophies and religions deny either permanence or change. Plato, the first great philosopher, called the things of this world which are subject to change "shadows." These "shadows" are only copies of the "reals" which are not subject to change. These "ideas" or "reals" are alone knowable and ultimately the truth. The things of this world cannot be known but are subject merely to different opinions. This world in which we live is not really real!

Though Plato had a false separation between appearance and reality, numerous other perspectives also have denied the essential realness of the physical world. Philosophic idealisms, be they Platonic or not, tend to undermine the reality of the physical world if they do not actually deny its reality. Mysticisms, be they philosophic or religious, usually deny the changing flux for unchanging Being, identified as "the One," or "the Real." This is especially true of Buddhism and Hinduism in the East as well as Western religions such as Christian Science influenced by the thought of nineteenth century idealism. But it is Plato, more than anyone else, that has frequently influenced Christianity to undervalue the reality of the physical. This can be most clearly seen in the Middle Ages when Christianity became very dualistic. Church music became a spiritual chant without words because the unchanging God was "beyond" such literalness, monasteries were born to separate spiritual pursuits from physical necessities, and spiritual leaders were forbidden to marry. But this unbalanced split is still too often with us today! This is particularly true in conservative Christianity. We emphasize the importance of salvation but neglect man's physical needs as if he is only spirit and not body.

9

Amos called down God's wrath upon those who may have continued a religious exercise, but cared little for the real human and physical needs of others. Our stress on Christian vocation for our young people often makes it sound like engineers and mechanics, or lawyers and doctors, are second-class citizens. Our individualistic and spiritual concerns within the church for the past fifty to sixty years have frequently lost sight of the universally moral and social implications of the Christian faith. The growth of naturalism and humanism in our country may partially be the indirect product of our myopic and bifurcated vision.

While this denial of the meaning and reality of the physical has thus been the danger of many religions and some philosophies, other philosophies do the opposite and deny the reality of the spiritual or non-physical. Now only nature exists. Everything changes! There is nothing permanent. Religions usually do not say this. But their frequently unbalanced emphasis on the spiritual and permanent to the exclusion, if not the denial, of physical and changing reality has often prompted the non-religious to the opposite extreme. This is particularly true in the "Christian" West. Contemporary existentialism as well as more optimistic expressions of naturalism and/or humanism are examples of the world-view of modern atheism. Christian liberalism, though certainly not atheistic, frequently understands reality in similar terms and thus promotes nearly the same ethic. Francis Schaeffer has pointed out that the word God for some theologians no longer has any real content but is used simply as a connotation or emotional word to provoke a pseudo-religious experience in which nothing definite can be said and in which rationality ultimately has no place.[1] But a true biblical balance leaves us with neither the extreme of denying this world for God, nor an affirmation of the world and man at the cost of a real and true knowledge of God.

Christian ontology begins by accepting two realities: the absolute independent, and sovereign God and the contingent, dependent, but real creation that exists outside of and in addition to, but never separate from, God. Reality is not a pantheism, but nevertheless it is both God and creation, both spirit and nature, both permanence and change. The Bible begins here--"in the beginning God created the heavens and the earth" (Genesis 1:1). Reality is neither monistic, nor pluralistic, but it is twofold, if not

10

actually dualistic. God is the only truly ultimate reality; nature, man, and everything other than God has been created ex nihilo as Augustine stated, or in other words, "out of nothing." This is not a new position, but follows the historic path of established doctrine; but it is in need of re-emphasis in our day due to the many philosophic and theological positions that tend to either deny or swallow up one reality within the other.

Both realities must be maintained. Nearly all other facets of biblical balance, be it God's special revelation to man, the inspiration of the Bible, the dignity and depravity of man, the provision and acceptance of salvation, etc., are all rooted in and simply are expressions of these two absolutely different realities. Without the real existence of nature and man as totally other than God there would be no need or possibility of revelation, and no provision of salvation since nature, man, and God would be ultimately one and the same. The reality of evil would be denied as it is in many Eastern philosophies and religions for good and evil cannot really be one and thus identical if language is really to be significant. Lastly, from a Christian perspective, there could logically be no unique incarnation for all men are already a part of God.

God and the created world are thus two different realities. Though there is a steady and non-arbitrary relationship between God and created reality, there is nothing close to equality, let alone identity. Isaiah 40:18-25 is one of many passages of the Bible that present the absolute and intrinsic uniqueness of God:

> To whom then will you liken God?
> Or what likeness will you compare
> with Him?
> As for the idol, a craftsman casts
> it,
> A goldsmith plates it with gold,
> And a silversmith fashions chains
> of silver.
>
> He who is too impoverished for such
> an offering
> Selects a tree that does not rot;
> He seeks out for himself a skillful
> craftsman
> To prepare an idol that will not
> totter.

11

Do you not know?   Have you not
    heard?
Has it not been declared to you
    from the beginning?
Have you not understood from the
    foundations of the earth?
It is He who sits above the vault
    of the earth,
And its inhabitants are like
    grasshoppers,
Who stretches out the heavens like
    a curtain
And spreads them out like a tent to
    dwell in.
He it is who reduces rulers to
    nothing,
Who makes the judges of the earth
    meaningless,
Scarcely have they been planted,
Scarcely have they been sown,
Scarcely has their stock taken root
    in the earth,
But He merely blows on them, and
    they wither,
And the storm carries them away
    like stubble.
"To whom then will you liken Me
That I should be his equal?" says
    the Holy One.

"To whom then will you liken Me that I should be
equal?" The obvious and implied answer is no one!
Nothing is comparable to or with God. Not only is
everything fallen and thus cursed with sin contrary to
God's holiness, but even before sin nothing was or
could be equal with God. God is the creator of
everything else. God, in other words, is One of a
kind, or put differently, is in an absolute class by
Himself. God alone is eternal, ever-living, self-
existent (Psalm 90:2; Isaiah 57:15; Jeremiah 10:10;
John 5:26; 1 Timothy 1:17). Everything else has come
into existence and is dependent on Him for continued
existence. This is why God answered Moses' inquiry of
His name as recorded in Exodus 3:14 with "'I AM WHO I
AM'; and He said, 'Thus you shall say to the sons of
Israel, "I AM has sent me to you."'" On the level of
existence, nothing is identical and thus nothing is
comparable or can be used as a complete analogy to
provide us knowledge of God's endless self-existence.
We do, of course, understand existence by the very fact

12

of our own existence. When a child is born we understand that the new presence of the child is evident of what we know as existence. Similarly, when one dies, we perceive the absence of our friend or loved one and realize what non-existence, at least physically, means. Therefore, we know what it means to say "God exists," if we do not comprehend what it means to be self-existent as every existent thing we know is dependent on its surrounding environment and its own metabolism.

God, then, is not only the self-existing reality, but also the permanent and unlimited (infinite) reality. Since ultimate reality demands permanence, God is the absolutely permanent reality. Malachi 3:6 records God's pronouncement that "I, the LORD, do not change." James 1:17 more pictorially depicts God's permanence as "no variation, or shifting shadow." (See also Psalm 102:27; Hebrews 13:8.) This essential, spiritual, and moral perfection is what the theologian calls God's immutability. Immutability does not mean a static or uncaring God as some imagine when they think of an immutable or unchanging reality. It simply means God's nature and character do not change. God cannot cease to exist. He has always been and will always be. He is holy and cannot be other than absolutely holy. This unchanging permanence is well-described by the great Baptist theologian, Augustus H. Strong:

> Reason teaches us that no change is possible in God, whether of increase or decrease, progress or deterioration, contraction or development. All change must be to better or worse. But God is absolute perfection, and no change to better is possible. Change to worse would be equally inconsistent with perfection.[2]

God is not only unchanging permanence, but absolutely unlimited. This does not mean He is unlimited only in regard to space or time, but more importantly, He is unlimited in regard to His Personal resources. He is transcendent!--beyond anything and everything else. The Psalmist states that "Great is the LORD, and highly to be praised; and His greatness is unsearchable" (Psalm 145:3). Speaking of what we call omnipotence and omniscience (all-powerful, all-knowing), Psalm 147:5 says that "great is our Lord, and abundant in strength; His understanding is infinite."

13

Job 11:7-11 also vividly describes the immeasurableness of the very being of God.

God's infinity means that God was and is absolutely self-sufficient. As we shall see in the next chapter, God exists as three-in-one Personhood, or trinity. God is thus self-sufficient not only for existence and in His omniscience and omnipotence, but also socially or personally. Creation was not necessary for God to experience fellowship. Fellowship basically means relationship among equals and thus complete theistic fellowship must be within God and not found outside of God in His creation. We shall speak further of this in the following chapter, but enough has been said to be able to state that <u>creation was neither a logical nor factual necessity</u>. Creation was an act of God's absolute freedom. Creation was not done because of some need or lack on the part of the absolute and perfect God, or He would not be absolute and perfect.

This means that God's grace permits something to exist in its own right and to be of both interest and value in its own right as well. We might say that God has renounced being the only existent. There is thus factually necessary and independent existence--God; and there is now also contingent and dependent existence--the created realm of nature and man.[3] This creation reality in no manner or form restricts God because of its own power or worth. However, this does not necessitate an arbitrary or irregular relationship between God and creation. Rather God has chosen to limit His freedom via the laws of nature and the laws of thought (logic) which are constant not only within nature and the world of man, but also in the dynamic between the transcendent God and the created domains of nature and humanity. The principles of logic and the laws of nature "are imposed on the scientific mind by the immanent rationality of the universe."[4] This rational structure of both nature and man is the creative product of the all-knowing God. As Dr. Torrance continues:

> The doctrine of creation out of nothing and of the continual preservation of creation from lapsing back into nothing . . . grounded the ongoing order of the universe in the steadfast love and faithfulness of God, which gave it

a stability as well as freedom in
its contingency, for it meant that
its natural liability was under-
girded by God himself.5

Thus while the created realities of man and nature
in no way limit or restrict God by their own being,
this does not mean that God has not limited Himself by
creation. God has ordered His space-time universe and
is fully aware that the shortest distance beween two
points is a straight line and that there are twenty-
four time zones on our planet. The incarnate Christ
experientially realized these and other God-ordained
laws of created and dependent nature. God's self-
imposed limitation of Himself because of His absolutely
holy nature and truthfulness can be most clearly seen
in the incident recorded in Exodus 32:9-14. Here we
find Moses interceding with God on behalf of idolatrous
and wicked Israel so that Israel might not be totally
destroyed. The basis of Moses' intercession is God's
Word of covenant with Abraham and the fact "it is
impossible for God to lie" (Hebrews 6:18). Thus while
God could physically destroy Israel and in no way could
be hindered or stopped by the Israelites themselves, He
cannot because of His covenant promise. It is thus
God's nature, will, and word that limit God in regard
to His wayward creatures and not they themselves, but
nevertheless their reality and relative freedom, if
here negatively expressed, is still graphically
portrayed.

Creation--be it nature per se or man--must not be
made into a shadow of reality as Plato did to the
things of this world nearly 2,400 years ago. Christianity is not physical-denying. "The earth is the
Lord's, and all it contains, the world, and those who
dwell in it" (Psalm 24:1). "For God is the king of all
the earth" and thus everything is God's! (Psalm 47:7).
And therefore everything is mine as the newborn child
of God. However, because of the inheritance of Adam's
sinful nature, humanity misuses the earth and does not
will God's will for either himself or the created
nature of which he was made steward and caretaker
(Genesis 1:28-30). But now as a believer in which all
things have become new the Christian must recognize and
give proper due to both himself as God's expressly
created and redeemed person and to nature as his God-
given responsibility, remembering that "all things have
been created" by and for our Lord Jesus Christ and that
"He is before all things, and in Him all things hold

15

together" (Colossians 1:16, 17). This is the Christian perspective of reality: a Creator and Sustainer of all things--the Lord Jesus, and the "realness" of what God has physically created to be enjoyed, controlled, studied, and rightfully used by his children. Any perspective that denies these realities of the eternal God and the dependent creation is what Paul means when he writes that we are to be taken "captive . . . according to Christ" and not by "philosophy and empty deception, according to the tradition of men" such as first-century Gnostics and other viewpoints that tend to deny the reality of either the physical or non-physical dimensions of reality. Such viewpoints are not according to the biblical principles and realities of balance (Colossians 2:8).

The secular humanism and scientific naturalism rampant in our day <u>are</u> <u>not</u> <u>balanced</u>. They have only half-the-pie, the half that is unintelligible in its own right. Nature is not self-explanatory. Man is not really given his proper dignity as simply a product of chance over innumerable aeons. While humanism makes man a god, humans are really ultimately no different than the other facets of evolving nature--animate or inanimate. There is no meaning to existence. No purpose to our unique personhood. It is no wonder that the result of such an outlook is seemingly culminating in our day in the same lawlessness of the ancient days in Israel when "everyone did what was right in his own eyes" (Judges 17:6; 21:25). Abortion on demand does not enhance the meaning and value of man. In many cases, highly bred farm animals are given more care and significance than human fetuses or even malformed infants. The most abnormal sexual relations are legitimized between "consenting adults" as we practice "what is right in our own eyes" for there is no God to see. God is dead, or never existed, and thus "man is nothing else but what he makes of himself."[6] The first chapter of Romans is relived as humanity "professes to be wise but becomes fools" as individuals have "exchanged the truth of God for a lie, and worshipped and served the creature rather than the Creator" and thus God has given them "over in the lusts of their hearts to impurity, that their bodies might be dis-honored among them" (Romans 1:24, 25).

Conservative and biblical Christianity in America frequently talks and acts as if we too have only half-the-pie, the essential and primary half no doubt, but still only half! Given the doctrine of creation,

16

however, the Christian cannot understand God correctly in total neglect of humanity, history, or nature. Man, created in God's image, is the absolutely unique creative revelation of God. But nature is also God's creation and we learn of "His invisible attributes, His eternal power and divine nature . . . through what has been made" (Romans 1:20). This is natural revelation, different from the philosophic development of natural theology in that it is not a logical proof of God's existence but an inference that there is indeed an infinite artist in light of the reality of His finite canvas. Natural revelation is not sufficient in its own right, but it is the framework and setting for special revelation. The special revelation that is recorded and given to us in the Bible can be accepted and comprehended <u>only</u> in the context that nature, history and human individuals are real and therefore both meaningful and significant because all three come from and are purposed toward God. Christians, who unbiblically lapse into a Platonic perversion of Christianity that denies the importance of the physical body, the wise stewardship of wildlife and our natural resources, the social and political structures of our individual nation-states, and the active academic cultivation of God's truth wherever it is found (to name only a few facets of created reality), are also guilty of having only half-the-pie and thus too are unbalanced in the opposite direction of humanism and naturalism. Only the historic and orthodox balance that maintains the truth that "in the beginning God created the heavens and the earth" and "man in his own image" is truly biblical.

REFLECTION

1. Why is a Platonic perspective unbiblical?

2. In what way is theological liberalism perhaps more dangerous to biblical truth than atheistic philosophies?

3. How does the doctrine of creation aid our understanding of the perennial intellectual problem of permanence and change?

4. Discuss the concept of God's infinity.

5. Describe the respective freedoms of God and man in the context of their mutual and on-going relationship.

6. In what way may secular humanism and some expressions of Christianity be guilty of similar heresies?

7. Explain, in your own words, what biblical balance means in regard to nature, history, ethics, psychology, and sociology.

ENDNOTES

[1]See, for instance, the two following Francis Schaeffer books, _How Should We Then Live_ (Old Tappan, New Jersey: Fleming H. Revell, 1976), pp. 167-181 and _The God Who Is There_ (Chicago: Inter-Varsity Press, 1968), pp. 78-84.

[2]Augustus H. Strong, _Systematic Theology_, three volumes in one (Westwood, New Jersey: Fleming H. Revell, 1962 reprint of 1907 original), p. 257.

[3]We are here dealing only with physical/terrestrial creation. Obviously, there is also a spirit/celestial creation that is also totally dependent on God for original and continued existence.

[4]Thomas Forsyth Torrance, _The Ground and Grammar of Theology_ (Charlottesville: University of Virginia Press, 1980), p. 51.

[5]_Ibid._, p. 58.

[6]Jean-Paul Sartre, _Existentialism and Human Emotions_ (New York: Philosophical Library, 1957), p. 15. Existentialism, while beginning at the same place as secular humanism and other optimistic naturalistic perspectives, is rightly pessimistic. Sartre wrote: "Dostoievsky said, 'If God didn't exist everything would be possible.' That is the very starting point of existentialism," p. 22. For a vigorous attack against secular humanism and scientific naturalisms such as Alfred North Whitehead's process philosophy, see the author's _Religious Ministry in a Transcendentless Culture_ (Washington, D.C.: University Press of America, 1980).

CHAPTER III

GOD: BOTH ONE AND MANY

Probably no biblical doctrine is more far reaching in its implications, or more difficult in its explanation, than the doctrine of the Trinity. This brief exposition will certainly not solve all the perceived cognitive problems, nor ease the perplexity of its conceptualization. Our purpose is, however, two-fold: first, to note the abundance of the Scriptural data that precluded non-trinitarian conclusions for historic orthodoxy; and secondly, to indicate that the trinitarian understanding of God alone answers the perennial intellectual problem of the relationship of the one and the many, or unity and diversity, demonstrating that this is not a man-made problem but rightly anticipates the essence of ultimate reality.

In light of this two-fold purpose, one very important distinction must be noted. Theologians speak of the ontological or essential Trinity and the economical or revelational Trinity. By this they are differentiating between the way God is in Himself and the way in which Scripture reveals God as Father, Son, and Holy Spirit. We are concerned here primarily with the latter; however, to understand ultimate reality as inherently One and Many is to absolutely confirm the ontological Trinity. While we can only speak of God to the degree in which He has revealed Himself, thus eliminating much metaphysical and theological speculation, we must assume and believe that in the nature of the one God there _are_ three eternal distinctions or revelation of God is not actually revelation. Therefore, we are on safe and non-speculative ground in calling attention to _both_ God's absolute unity in essence _and_ diversity in distinction as the answer to philosophy's vain but not meaningless quest.

The primary stumbling-block for many individuals in regard to the Trinity is a perceived discrepancy between Judaism and Christianity, or the Old Testament and the New Testament. However, there are many intimations of plurality within the Godhead in the Old Testament. By themselves these intimations do not furnish a clear or sufficient basis for the doctrine apart from New Testament revelation. However, they certainly do not contradict the New Testament but rather implicitly confirm it through the many nuances of statement and hinted plurality.

One such intimation of divine plurality is the Hebrew word for God (Elohim). This Hebrew application of the plural to God is frequently explained as a plural of majesty or unlimited greatness. This may well be the case. But it very possibly may be the case that the word was originally chosen by the Holy Spirit because it alluded to a plurality in the divine nature. Many of the early Church Fathers saw an allusion to the Trinity in the biblical use of this word. Augustus H. Strong notes that the Holy Spirit's probable use of this word was "with a view to the future unfolding of truth with regard to the Trinity."[1]

This cannot and need not be settled here. The case for intimation of the plurality of the divine nature in the Old Testament is affected very little, if at all, by the meaning and use of this word. More important is God's frequent use of plural pronouns in referring to Himself, often in conjunction with Elohim. For instance, in Genesis 1:26 we read that "God said, 'Let Us make man in Our image, according to Our likeness . . .'" [italics added]. Similarly, we read in Genesis 3:22, after the Fall, that the "Lord God said, ' Behold, the man has become like one of Us . . .'" [italics added]. At Babel, we are told in Genesis 11:7 that God said "Let Us go down and there confuse their language . . ." [italics added]. This use of plural pronouns to describe Himself is not limited to the first twelve chapters of Genesis. One of the greatest of the Hebrew prophets, Isaiah, hears after his transcendent vision this question addressed to him by God: "Whom shall I send, and who will go for Us?" [italics added]. All of these references seemingly refer to plurality and not majesty or greatness as may be the case for the word Elohim. In this latter verse, and to some extent in each reference, the unity and diversity of the Godhead is expressed. Here in Isaiah both singular and plural pronouns are used to refer to the same subject--"whom shall I send, and who will go for Us?" John Calvin long ago wrote that he was "rather favorable to the opinion that this passage points to three Persons in the Godhead" because "God talks with himself, and in the plural number."[2] While Calvin might be dismissed out of hand by Unitarians and Jewish believers, there really does not seem to be any reasonable understanding of these Old Testament references other than at least the plurality, if not the triunity, of the Godhead. Any other interpretation such as the inclusion of angels in the use of the plural pronouns would seemingly do injustice to the literal interpretation of Scripture as well as equating

22

the angels with God, especially in the moral capacity
of distinguishing good from evil in Genesis 3:22.

The Old Testament also distinguishes the Spirit of
God from God. This distinguishing between God and the
Spirit of God can be seen in the task of creation in
Genesis 1:1, 2. It is more clearly seen in Isaiah
48:16 where the Redeemer, the Holy One of Israel,
states that "the Lord GOD has sent Me, and His Spirit."
Though this is not explicitly trinitarian in itself, it
most certainly is complementary as the Redeemer in
biblical thought is ultimately God Himself. Without
doubt there are three individuals in view here. Very
similarly, Isaiah 61:1, 2 speaks of the Spirit of the
Lord GOD being upon the anointed one. Christ (meaning
anointed) applies this passage to Himself in Luke 4:18.
Jesus is the anointed One, the Christ, or in Hebrew,
Messiah! As we shall see, the Messiah is also
Immanuel--God is with us. Seen in the light of New
Testament passages that speak of both Jesus Christ and
the Holy Spirit as absolutely one with God, these
references in Isaiah are very supportive of not simply
plurality as in the use of the name _Elohim_, or plural
pronouns, but the Trinity per se.[3]

There are two other Old Testament concepts that
would appear to necessitate a plural differentiation
within the Godhead: the Messianic Sonship and the
Angel of the Lord passages. In Psalm 2:7 we read that
"Thou art My Son, Today I have begotten Thee." This is
certainly compatible with the New Testament revelation
that announces the Sonship of Jesus. The promise of a
virgin conceiving and bearing a Son, named "Immanuel,"
or "God is with us" (Isaiah 7:14), is definitely
identified by Matthew as pertaining to the birth of
Jesus (Matthew 1:23). Likewise, Jesus' indirect claim
to eternality that "before Abraham was born, I am"
(John 8:58) totally agrees with Micah 5:2 that states
in regard to Bethlehem that "One will go forth for Me
to be ruler in Israel. His goings forth are from long
ago." The eternal Son of Psalm 2:7 must be identical
with the One from "long ago" in Micah who is "to be
ruler in Israel," and the promised child of Isaiah 7:14
whose name is to be "Immanuel." Jesus' statement
concerning His own pre-existence and implied eternality
identifies Him not only with Isaiah 7:14 via Matthew,
but also with Micah and particularly Psalm 2:7 in light
of Psalm 45:6 that is directly referred to Him in
Hebrews 1:8: "Thy throne, O God, is forever and ever."
Can there, then, be any real doubt for one who accepts
the Bible that the promised child of Isaiah 9:6 whose
"Name will be called Wonderful, Counselor, Mighty God,

Eternal Father, Prince of Peace" is one-and-the-same Person with Paul's statement in Galatians 4:4 that "when the fulness of the time came, God sent forth His Son, born of a woman, born under the Law"?

The last facet of the Old Testament record that would appear to suggest plurality in the Godhead is the various appearances of the "angel [messenger] of the Lord" who not only identifies himself with God but accepts worship due only to God. Abraham, for instance, is addressed by the angel of the Lord on Mt. Moriah when he is about to sacrifice Isaac as recorded in Genesis 22. In verse 12 the angel says not only "I know that you fear God," but also, because of that fear "you have not withheld your son, your only son, from Me" [italics added]. Abraham was not offering Isaac to an angel, but God, and thus the angel of the Lord _must_ _be_ _God_ if the angel states that Isaac was not being withheld from himself. In even more direct fashion, Jacob is addressed by the angel of the Lord in Genesis 31:11 who identifies himself as "the God of Bethel, where you anointed a pillar, where you made a vow to Me" in verse 13. These two incidents not only make the messenger one who is _sent_ _from_ _God_, but also one who in some manner is _identical_ _and_ _equal_ _to_ _God_! This revelation of the Person of God may not be as explicit and direct as the New Testament in regard to the distinctions within the Godhead, but it certainly is not obscure when read in light of the culmination of revelation, Jesus Christ. Jesus Christ Who is sent and separate from God the Sender, but also identical with and equally called God by God (Hebrews 1:1-8).

Perhaps the most distinctive revelation of God prior to the incarnation of Jesus Christ was the appearance of God as the angel of the Lord to Moses. This is the event in which God is revealed as the covenant God and identifies Himself as "I am" or "Yahweh." In Exodus 3:3 we are told that "the _angel_ _of_ _the_ _Lord_ appeared to him [Moses] in a blazing fire from the _midst_ _of_ _the_ _bush_" and in verse 4 that "_God_ called to him from the _midst_ _of_ _the_ _bush_" [italics added]. Not only is this rather straight forward identification of the angel with God, but in verse 5 Moses is given instructions to remove his sandals because "the place on which you are standing is holy ground." Angels may be sinless, even holy, but they are not to be worshipped because they too are created beings. Therefore the injunction for Moses to worship this One provides us positive proof of His divinity. The final proof is when the figure in the bush declares Himself to be "the God of your father, the God of Abraham, the

24

God of Isaac, and the God of Jacob" (verse 6). Moses responded properly for he then "hid his face, for he was afraid to look at God."[4] Certainly in this passage, and in other similar angel of the Lord passages, the messenger is both separate from but identical with God. No relationship is more similar to this separate but identical relationship of the angel of the Lord and God than the relationship of Father and Son in the New Testament (John 10:30; 12:45; 14:9). Nor is any explanation more feasible than the doctrine of the Trinity to comprehend separate entities but essential identity, be it the Father/Son relationship of the New Testament or the angel of the Lord/God relationship in the Old Testament. It is no surprise that Lewis Sperry Chafer notes the "unanimity of belief on the part of all devout scholars that the Angel of Jehovah is the preincarnate second Person of the Trinity."[5]

This being the case, at least from the hindsight of New Testament revelation, it may be difficult for young Christians to understand or empathize with a Jewish believer who perceives the doctrine of the Trinity as idolatry. We must do two things. First, attempt to read the passages enumerated in this chapter as if you were totally ignorant of the New Testament and thus the Person of Jesus Christ. Would you come to a conclusion similar to the doctrine of the Trinity on your own? Or would you wish for a clearer description and fuller explanation of passages that hint at the plurality of God and the dynamics of Yahweh and His Angel? Secondly, we must make an attempt to realize the effect which the _Shema_ has on the religious mentality of the average Jew. Jewish people often object to the triunity of God _because_ of what they believe the _Shema_ teaches. The _Shema_ is simply the foundational passage for historical Judaism. Jesus Himself identifies it as the first commandment (Mark 12:29, 30).

> Hear, O Israel! The Lord is our
> God, the Lord is one! And you
> shall love the Lord your God with
> all your heart and with all your
> soul and with all your might
> (Deuteronomy 6:4, 5).

For most Jewish people the _Shema_ is the very center of Judaism. The word _Shema_ is the first Hebrew word in this passage and simply means "hear." The passage is understood as saying that God is indivisibly one and therefore the Christian claim that Jesus Christ is God is impossible and blasphemous. However, when careful attention is paid to the Hebrew text and the meaning of the word "one" (echad), the Shema becomes one of the strongest statements in support of the plurality of God and thus the distinct possibility of the Trinity--Father, Son, and Holy Spirit.

The word for "one" (echad) is the word that is always used to describe plurality in unity. For instance, this is the word in Genesis 2:24 to describe the unity of husband and wife as "one flesh." Similarly, the return of the twelve spies with their very large but "single (echad) cluster of grapes" is a very distinctive compound unity.[6] Thus while the use of echad in Deuteronomy 6:4 does not prove the doctrine of the Trinity, it most surely does express and convey the obvious possibility of the compound unity of God as the Christian doctrine of the Trinity affirms.

It should be mentioned that absolute oneness or singularity could have been expressed in Deuteronomy 6:4 by the word yachid. It is frequently translated "only" as it is in Genesis 22:2 to refer to Isaac as the only son of promise.[7] The word, however, is never used of God. Thus while the Hebrew had two words to convey unity, compounded or absolute, the Holy Spirit's total preference for the word which identifies plurality with God seems to leave little doubt as to the intention of Scriptural revelation. Thus since echad means oneness in plurality and the doctrine of the Trinity means exactly this in regard to the divine Unity subsisting in three Persons or Distinctions, Deuteronomy 6:4 does not exclude or contradict Christian teaching but may be easily understood as directly reinforcing it and may even be one of the strongest statements in support of the tri-unity in the entire Bible.[8]

The tri-unity of God speaks directly to the philosophical problem of unity and diversity. This is the problem that the very first philosophers tried to solve by stating that "all is water" or "all is air," etc. Realizing that these were not adequate solutions, Plato put forward his theory of ideas. By this he meant that the many entities we see on earth are really only copies of one ideal model. Empirical images are subject to opinion and thus reason (logic) is the way to knowledge of the ideas. For Plato, this ideal model was the solution to the questions of plurality and impermanence since these were true of the "images" of the idea that we perceive, but the "idea" itself was singular and immutable.

26

Many in the history of thought have put forward various forms of philosophic idealism. Most have struggled with the same metaphysical and epistemological issues that Plato had. Baruch (Benedict) de Spinoza (1632-1677) was concerned with the certainty of knowledge following a geometric model, but the idealism that resulted also solved the unity/diversity question in a manner that seemingly sacrificed plural diversity for the sake of ultimate unity in what Spinoza named "God" or "nature." Spinoza labeled himself a pantheist. Thinkers more religious than Spinoza attempt to solve the unity and diversity problem by making everything finally unified by being a part of God. This solution is not a possibility for Bible believers. God created real entities <u>outside</u> <u>and</u> <u>different</u> <u>from</u> Himself! But though all philosophic solutions to this problem of the one and the many have been found to be inadequate, this does not mean the philosophers have created an intellectual problem that really does not exist. Rather the very source of reality is <u>both</u> <u>one</u> <u>and</u> <u>many</u>. Unity and diversity is the very essence of ultimate reality. God is three-and-yet-one! As Francis Schaeffer remarks:

> Every once in a while in my
> discussions someone asks how I can
> believe in the Trinity. My answer
> is always the same. I would still
> be an agnostic if there were no
> Trinity, because there would be no
> answers. Without the high order of
> personal unity and diversity as
> given in the Trinity, <u>there</u> <u>are</u> <u>no</u>
> <u>answers</u> [original italics].9

Thus the Christian cannot reject the "both/andness" of the doctrine of the Trinity because it is difficult and seemingly impossible to conceptualize. Not only is it a biblical doctrine, it is the very reason people have struggled for so long with the one and many, or unity and diversity, question. This is the way reality <u>really</u> <u>is</u>. God's love existed and was expressed before the creation of man as it was shared between the Persons of the Trinity throughout eternity past. Jesus states this in His high priestly prayer--"Thou didst love Me before the foundation of the world" (John 17:24). "God is love" (1 John 4:16) means that God has to be thought of as a community whose very essence and freedom are expressed by self-giving love. Creation was thus not a necessity so that God might have personal relationships and someone to love. The Trinity is self-sufficient personally and

27

emotionally (if we may so speak) as well as in regard to existence and holiness. The doctrine of the Trinity is our second example that seemingly contradictory facets of a theological truth must both be held to be faithful to the biblical message. Theological conservatives need not fear biblical balance, then, when it is introduced in regard to revelation, inspiration, testamental continuity, salvation, last things and other truths in subsequent pages. For God is both one and many--Father, Son, and Holy Spirit.

REFLECTION

1. Why must the ontological and revelational Trinity be essentially identical for a biblical Christian?

2. Discuss the intimations of the plurality of God in the vocabulary and grammar of the Old Testament.

3. Interpret Isaiah 48:16 and 61:1, 2 in regard to the possibility of God's plurality.

4. Read the following Old Testament verses and correlate their teaching: Psalm 2:7; Isaiah 7:14; Micah 5:2. Relate these to New Testament passages such as Matthew 1:23; John 8:58; Hebrews 1:1-8.

5. Discuss the seeming implications of the following verses: Genesis 22:11-12; Exodus 3:3-6; Judges 13:8-23.

6. How may Francis Schaeffer claim that the doctrine of the Trinity saved him from agnosticism?

[1]Augustus H. Strong, Systematic Theology, three volumes in one (Westwood, New Jersey: Fleming H. Revell Company, 1962 reprint of 1907 original), p. 319.

[2]John Calvin, Calvin's Commentaries, Isaiah (Grand Rapids: A & P Publishers, n.d.), III, 92.

[3]See, for instance, John 1:1-4, 18; 3:16; 5:22, 23; 8:58; 17:4, 24; Colossians 1:15-17; Hebrews 1:8 for an example of the direct identity of Jesus as the co-eternal and co-equal God as Son. The Holy Spirit is equally seen as co-substantial with the Father and the Son in such New Testament references as Matthew 12:31, 32; 28:19; Acts 5:3, 4; 1 Corinthians 2:10, 11; 12:4-6; 2 Corinthians 3:16-18; 13:14; Hebrews 9:14.

[4]A very similar occurrence, even to the removal of one's sandals and the bowing down in worship, happened to Joshua when the "captain of the host of the LORD" appeared to him, indicating again at least a duality in the Godhead (Joshua 5:13-15). Note also the appearance of the angel of the Lord to Manoah and his fear of death because "we have seen God" (Judges 13:18-22).

[5]Lewis Sperry Chafer, Systematic Theology (Dallas: Dallas Seminary Press, 1964), I, 327.

[6]Other uses of echad that is singular and yet plural are seen in Ezra's use of it to speak to "the whole assembly numbered 42,360" (Ezra 2:64) and Jeremiah's use of this word to express the compound unity of an entire nation having "one heart and one way" (Jeremiah 32:39).

[7]See Judges 11:34; Psalm 22:20; Proverbs 4:3; Jeremiah 6:26; Amos 8:10; and Zechariah 12:10.

[8]There remains yet some question as to whether Deuteronomy 6:4 even refers to the unity of God but rather simply states that He alone is God. This ambiguity can be seen in the possible translations the NIV suggests: "The Lord our God is one Lord"; or "The Lord is our God, the Lord is one"; or "the Lord is our God, the Lord alone." Only the first two alternatives, seemingly suggesting God's unity, would understand echad as "unity in plurality."

[9]Francis Schaeffer, He Is There And He Is Not Silent (Wheaton, Illinois: Tyndale House Publishers, 1972), p. 14.

CHAPTER IV

CHRIST: BOTH DIVINE AND HUMAN

Closely associated with the doctrine of the Trinity, both biblically and historically, is the question as to the identity and nature of the Person of Christ. The Trinity doctrine developed because of the necessity to express how Jesus was God and yet in another sense was not the totality of the Godhead. The New Testament certainly claims that Jesus is God and other than God. In addition to the many direct claims of Jesus Himself such as "before Abraham was born, I am" (John 8:58) and "He who has seen Me has seen the Father" (John 14:9), there is the prologue of the Gospel of John:

> In the beginning was the Word, and the Word was with God, and the Word was God. He was in the beginning with God. All things come into being by Him, and apart from Him nothing came into being that has come into being. . . . And the Word became flesh, and dwelt among us, and we beheld His glory, glory as of the only begotten from the Father, full of grace and truth (John 1:1-3, 14).

Jesus, most definitely, is seen here as God and yet with God. John also states that the Word Who was God also "became flesh." The literal meaning of the word "incarnation" is simply "enfleshment." God became man! Immanuel of Isaiah 7:14 is Jesus of Nazareth, Mary's uniquely virgin born Son (Matthew 1:22-25), "being supposedly the son of Joseph" (Luke 3:23). This biblical data raised two theological problems for both the early church and for Christians of every era: first, how was Christ both divine and human? and secondly, what was the relationship between Jesus Christ identified by Matthew as Immanuel (God with us) and God? This latter question, as we have seen, was comprehended by the doctrine of the Trinity, a non-biblical word perhaps, but certainly a biblical doctrine that agreed with even the Old Testament's expression and incipient understanding of the plurality of the Godhead. Our attention, therefore, in this chapter is with the first question.

31

The very first attempts at answering this question usually took one of the two possibilities, similar to evangelical and/or fundamentalist divisions today, but not the biblical balance of both. Some Jewish individuals came to regard Jesus as the last and greatest of the prophets, but not as the eternal Son of God since Jesus was the son of Joseph and Mary. Paul was rejected as an apostate Pharisee. Ebionites, as they were called (the word coming from Hebrew meaning "poor"), thus believed that Jesus was simply a great human teacher. Strong writes that "Ebionism was simply Judaism within the pale of the Christian Church, and its denial of Christ's Godhead was occasioned by the apparent incompatibility of this doctrine with monotheism."[1] Much of twentieth century Protestant liberalism has presented the same human Jesus.

The second position that rejected the biblical balance that Christ was both divine and human was Docetism. If Ebionism was Judaism within the church, Docetism was simply pagan philosophy in Christian clothes. Since physical matter was inherently evil, the Christ could not have a human body. Thus Docetism taught that Jesus Christ only "seemed" or "appeared" to have a body. (Their name came from the Greek word meaning "to seem," dokeo.) Ignatius, one of the very earliest of the Church Fathers having been martyred in the reign of Trajan (98-117), wrote vehemently against Docetism as well as the legalism of Ebionite type Judaizers ("if we still go on observing Judaism we admit we never received grace," Letter to the Magnesians, 8):

> [I] urge you to be thoroughly convinced of the birth, Passion and resurrection, which occurred while Pontius Pilate was governor (Letter to the Magnesians, 11).
>
> Regarding our Lord, you are absolutely convinced that on the human side he was actually sprung from David's line, Son of God according to God's will and power, actually born of a virgin, baptized by John, that "all righteousness might be fulfilled by him," and actually crucified for us in the flesh, under Pontius Pilate and

32

> Herod the Tetrarch. . . . And he
> genuinely suffered, as even he
> genuinely raised himself. It is
> not as some unbelievers say, that
> his Passion was a sham. It's they
> who are a sham! Yes, and their
> fate will fit their fancies--they
> will be ghosts and apparitions
> (Letter to the Smyraeans, 1).2

There were other later attempts to solve this
problem of Jesus' divinity and humanity. We need not
follow these historically here.3 It is worthwhile to
note, however, that the New Testament itself refutes
these half-way and thus totally false solutions.
Paul's attack on "philosophy and empty deception"
(Colossians 2:8) may be understood as a rejection of
either extreme. This is most obvious in Colossians
1:15, 22. In verse 15 Paul speaks of Christ being "the
image of the invisible God" and in verse 22 of the fact
that "He has now reconciled you in His fleshly body
through death." Obviously, Christ is more than a great
prophet as the "image of the invisible God," but He is
also more than a "phantom" if He possesses a "fleshly
body" susceptible to death. This two fold emphasis is
equally clear in the writings of John. John certainly
is fighting against both heresies of one or the other
extreme. His very words concerning the "Logos" in John
1:14 makes this quite plain--the Logos "became flesh."4
In the first two verses of his first epistle John
writes not only of Him Who was from the beginnings of
beginnings and was manifested or revealed to us, but
also that He was really physical in that we "beheld and
our hands handled" the Word of Life. For John,
therefore, the denial of either the full humanity
and/or deity of Jesus is an indication of the anti-
christian spirit that is already present:

> By this you know the Spirit of
> God: every spirit that confesses
> that Jesus Christ has come in the
> flesh is from God; and every spirit
> that does not confess Jesus is not
> from God; and this is the spirit of
> the antichrist, of which you have
> heard that it is coming, and now it
> is already in the world (1 John
> 4:2, 3) [italics added].

33

Perhaps the most definitive New Testament passage that provides us in clear relief the fact that Jesus, the Christ, is both divine and human is Philippians 2:5-8:

> Have this attitude in yourselves which was also in Christ Jesus, who, although He existed in the form of God, did not regard equality with God a thing to be grasped, but emptied Himself, taking the form of a bondservant, and being made in the likeness of men. And being found in appearance as a man, He humbled Himself by becoming obedient to the point of death, even death on a cross.

In looking at this passage we must remember that Paul's purpose is not theological. He is not purposefully attempting to explain to us the unique nature of Jesus Christ as both divine and human. The latter may be the result of his teaching, but his primary purpose is to provide us an example and model of the attitude of humility. A. B. Bruce states this in his excellent study entitled The Humiliation of Christ: "the apostle's purpose is not formally to teach that Christ was truly God, so that it was not arrogance on His part to claim equality of nature with God; but rather to teach that He being God did not make a point of retaining the advantageous connected with the divine state of being."[5] Paul thus desires to set before the Philippi church the mind of Christ rather than the self-seeking mind of fallen humanity since those associated with Christ should be slowly conforming "to the image of His Son" (Romans 8:29). As John the Baptist said, "He must increase, but I must decrease" (John 3:30).

This mind of humility is illustrated by both the self-emptying of "the form of God" by which Christ could become man, and the continuous state of humble obedience that culminated in "death on a cross." This self-emptying (kenosis theory) does not imply that Christ gave up any of His divine attributes. Neither His absolute attributes of holiness, truth, and love nor those related to creation such as omniscience, omnipotence, omnipresence, etc. To give up the divine attributes would be to give up the essence or character of God. Rather it seems best to speak of Christ giving

34

up the divine glory and the "independent exercise of
the relative attributes" (John 17:5; 2 Corinthians
8:9). The marginal reading of the NASV suggests the
phrase "laid aside his privileges" to convey the idea
of Christ's self-emptying in Philippians 2:7. In other
words, as a man, Jesus was not in Jerusalem and Galilee
at the same time. The "form of a bondservant" and the
"likeness of men" inherently prescribed the limits of
the God-man. This did not mean that He was no longer
in possession of, nor that He totally forsook the use
of, the divine attributes related to creation. It did
mean that His voluntary submission to the necessities
of being human were seen in His growing tired, becoming
hungry and/or thirsty, and lastly even weeping over
Lazarus. Jesus matured and developed as any other
human individual--physically, intellectually, socially,
and spiritually (Luke 2:40, 52).

The full humanity of Christ in no way detracted
from the total deity of our Lord. The first few verses
of the book of Hebrews is clear on this as well as
Philippians 2. Christ is there presented as the
culmination of the history of revelation because He is
"the exact representation of His nature" (Hebrews 1:3).
This identity with God was the case not only prior to
the incarnation, or when He had returned to heaven and
"sat down at the right hand of the Majesty on high,"
but also during the time when "He had made purification
of sins." This, of course, was accomplished on
Golgotha's tree as the incarnated God-man.

The phrase "the exact representation of His
nature" is primarily the translation, besides an
article and pronoun, of two Greek words. The word
translated nature (hypostasis) comes from two words
meaning "standing under" or "supporting." When used
metaphorically or philosophically rather than literally, it is best translated substance, nature, or
actual existence of something.6 It is the reality
itself. The other word (charakter) is the word that
was used to refer to the distinct engraven image on
coins.7 This is its sole New Testament usage and quite
clearly sets forth the idea that Jesus Christ is the
exact image or impression (literally "character") of
God. Marvin R. Vincent captures the use of these two
words here in regard to Christ's full deity while
incarnated when he writes that "the essential being of
God is conceived as setting its distinctive stamp upon
Christ, coming into definite and characteristic

35

expression in his person, so that the Son bears the exact impress of the divine nature and character."[8]

This being the case, what, then, is the "form" of God of which Christ emptied Himself? It cannot and must not be equated or identified with the divine nature. Strong writes that what the "Logos divested himself of, in becoming man, is not the substance of his Godhead but the 'form of God' in which this substance was manifested."[9] Vincent states that "the word is intended to describe that mode in which the essential being of God expresses itself."[10] "Form" (morphe) of God, then, is the manner or expression of being, but not being or essence itself. Nevertheless, only God has the expression or mode of existence as God. Likewise, Jesus is also in the "form" (morphe) or mode of existence of a bondservant (doulos). He thus veils His divine expression with a human one, though the veil is lifted briefly at the transfiguration (Luke 9:27-36). Christ thus emptied Himself by taking something to Himself--the manner and form of a servant. It is a change of state--the form of servant rather than the form of God. Since this word alludes to one's state or expression of being, the humiliation of Christ is expressed throughout the time of His sojourn on earth. His obedience, expressed in His prayer that "if it is possible, let this cup pass from Me, yet not as I will, but as Thou wilt" (Matthew 26:39) led to "death, even death on a cross." His voluntary humiliation of the cross is the final expression of His self-emptying! Thus His oneness with God was not to be clung to as if it could be lost or denied. He was equal to God because He "was God" (John 1:1).

If this passage tells us of Christ's essential deity as the absolute expression of God, it also speaks of his complete and full humanity. Two Greek words express His true humanity in verses 7 and 8. In verse 7 we read that He was "made in the likeness of men." This word "likeness" (homoiomati) refers to His "internal" similarity with humans. It is the word that the early church rejected as inappropriate to express Christ's relationship with God because it did not mean complete identity of nature. It is appropriate here, however, because Christ does not totally share man's nature--He is sinless. Nevertheless, Christ did walk and talk. He was a man--physically, emotionally, socially, cognitively, and spiritually. The New Testament gives us manifold evidence of this. His times of prayer give evidence of His true humanity

(Matthew 14:23; 26:36; Mark 6:46; 14:32; Luke 6:12; 9:28; 11:1; 22:41; John 14:16; 17:1-26). Muller writes that this "likeness" "denotes the human manner of existence into which Christ entered and which agrees with what in the divine sphere is called the 'existence in a manner equal to God.'"11 The result of the incarnation of God's Son is that He could be ignorant (Mark 13:32), tempted (Matthew 4:1-11), and could suffer and die (Matthew 27:33-60), not in regard to the divine nature but mediately by virtue of His human nature! These are the particular results of the self-limiting and self-emptying of the enfleshed God. Jesus is thus one with us even if not absolutely identical with us (Hebrews 2:17, 18). This is why Paul sees Christ in the likeness of "men" not "man" since Christ represents the human race. It is by the "grace of the one Man" that the grace of God may "abound to the many" (Romans 5:15). He is the Second Adam.

Christ could become a man because humanity was originally made in the image of God (Genesis 1:26, 27; 9:6). While Christ obviously veils His divine glory and voluntarily limits His infinity so as to be a particular man of Galilee, the incarnation is not an impossibility nor a logical contradiction. This is because of the inherent similarity of man with God, provided, of course, by God in creation. Just as there is a genuine, if general, revelation of God in man because we are made to have personal and moral relationship with God as personal and moral beings, so Christ can become man because man is originally personal, moral, even holy. Thus the Second Person of the Trinity does not lose His holiness in becoming man (Hebrews 4:15). He is simply what Adam was originally, and what we now are obligated to once again become-- holy. God's wrath is upon us because of our ungodliness and unrighteousness, i.e. lack of holiness (Romans 1:18). But the Second Adam, the One "who knew no sin" has become "sin on our behalf, that we might become the righteousness of God in Him" (2 Corinthians 5:21).

Not only was Jesus like men, but he was also "found in appearance as a man" (Philippians 2:8). This word (schemati) has to do with His outward appearance. He looked like any other male individual. Paul, with this word, desires to emphasize Christ's outward guise and demeanor. We see this illustrated with the Samaritan woman in John 4. From a distance she merely perceived a male figure to be at the well. Drawing closer, she realized Him to be a Jew (verse 9), and only after an intimate exchange did she realize that He was more than Jewish man, He was the long-awaited Messiah (verses 25, 26).

Philippians 2:5-8 leaves us no option between the deity and humanity of Jesus Christ if we are to accept the words of Scripture. Only the unique God-man can be our Redeemer. He is not only identified with the sinner (2 Corinthians 5:21; Hebrews 2:17, 18; 4:15), but is solely sufficient to be the eternal and final propitiation and covering of sin by satisfying God's righteousness with God's righteousness itself (Romans 3:24, 25; 1 Timothy 2:5; Hebrews 9:14).

Numerous other aspects of Jesus' life and the New Testament record provide additional evidence of both His deity and His humanity. The virgin birth, for instance, is necessitated because of His unique Personage. He must be born of a woman to really be part of the human race and thereby our Saviour. At the same time, He cannot be born in the normal manner for this would result in a person distinct from the incarnate Second Person of the Trinity. It is not surprising, therefore, that the New Testament frequently attributes human characteristics and action to this Person when He is referred to by a divine title (Romans 9:5; 1 Corinthians 2:8) and contrariwise, Christ's divine attributes and work are predicated of Him simultaneously with being given a human title (Acts 2:22-24; 17:31; Colossians 1:13, 14).

Jesus Christ is absolutely divine in light of the roles or offices the New Testament gives Him--Creator (Colossians 1:15-17), the final Judge (John 5:22, 23), and the forgiver of sins, even as incarnate (Mark 2:5, 10, 11). But the same New Testament, like Philippians, emphasizes Jesus' full humanity. There is no doubt that He is a complete human: body (Matthew 26:12), soul (Matthew 26:38), and spirit (Luke 23:46). Questions may yet remain concerning the personality and sinlessness of Jesus Christ. Some are answerable in books labeled systematic theologies, others will be answered only in God's presence. Nevertheless the biblical balance that we must always maintain is evident also in the Person of our Lord and Saviour. Jesus Christ is both divine and human. The Church Council at Chalcedon in 451 caught this biblical balance when it stated "Only-begotten, to be acknowledged in two natures . . . preserved and concurring in one Person and one subsistence . . . the

same Son, the Only-begotten, God the Word, the Lord
Jesus Christ."

REFLECTION

1. Discuss the two early extremes concerning the Person of Christ. How may we refute these teachings both biblically and logically?

2. What is Paul's main intention in Philippians 2:1-11? Apply this passage devotionally to your own life. Sketch a brief outline of this passage for just such devotional application as a teacher of God's Word.

3. Define the kenosis theory. Does this mean Christ relinquished any dimension of His deity? If not, what does it mean?

4. Before reviewing Philippians, demonstrate how Hebrews 1:3 sets forth the deity and humanity of Jesus Christ. What other New Testament indicators are there of Jesus' full deity and true humanity?

5. Explain the Greek word <u>morphe</u>. How does this word point to both Christ's deity and humanity in Philippians 2:6-8. What other distinct proof is there of Christ's complete humanity in this passage?

6. Why is the Virgin Birth a cardinal doctrine of true Christianity? Can one be saved and be ignorant of this doctrine? May a believer be doctrinally correct and reject this doctrine?

7. Discuss the historical and theological significance of the Chalcedonian Creed.

[1] A variant form of Gnosticism, labeled Cerinthianism after its founder, was similar to Ebionism in speaking of Jesus as a mere man who was uniquely endowed as the Christ by the Holy Spirit during the time between the baptism of Jesus and the crucifixion.

[2] Cyril C. Richardson (editor and translator), Early Christian Fathers, volume I in The Library of Christian Classics (Philadelphia: Westminster Press, 1953), pp. 96, 97, 113.

[3] There are many excellent history of doctrine books. A very excellent introductory text is L. Berkhof, The History of Christian Doctrine (Grand Rapids: William B. Eerdmans, 1937). A more exhaustive book is J. N. D. Kelly, Early Christian Doctrines, second edition (New York: Harper & Row, 1960).

[4] A. T. Robertson believes that John's phrase He "became flesh" is John's answer to those who denied the actual humanity of Christ or separated the Christ experience from the man Jesus, Word Pictures in the New Testament, five volumes (Nashville: Broadman Press, 1932), V, 4.

[5] A. B. Bruce, The Humiliation of Christ (New York: Hodder & Stoughton, n.d.), p. 17.

[6] Henry George Liddell and Robert Scott, A Greek-English Lexicon, ninth edition (Oxford: Clarendon Press, 1961), 1895.

[7] Ibid., p. 1977.

[8] Marvin R. Vincent, Word Studies in the New Testament, four volumes (Grand Rapids: William B. Eerdmans Publishing Company, 1946), IV, 383.

[9] Strong, op. cit., pp. 705-706.

[10] Vincent, op. cit., III, 431.

[11] Jac J. Muller, The Epistles of Paul to the Philippians and to Philemon in The New International Commentary on the New Testament, editor Ned B. Stonehouse (Grand Rapids: William B. Eerdmans Publishing Company, 1955), p. 82.

CHAPTER V

MAN: BOTH DIGNIFIED AND DEPRAVED

It is dangerous to make men
see too clearly his equality with
the brutes without showing him his
greatness. It is also dangerous to
make him see his greatness too
clearly, apart from his vileness.
It is still more dangerous to leave
him in ignorance of both. But it
is very advantageous to show him
both. Man must not think that he
is on a level either with the
brutes or with the angels, nor must
he be ignorant of both sides of his
nature; but he must know both.[1]

Blaise Pascal's balance in the seventeenth century
is the same balance we seek for contemporary American
Christianity. Pascal is absolutely correct when he
asserts that we must know both sides of our nature.
But American Christianity has much too frequently taken
only one side to the functional, if not the theoretical, exclusion of the other side. Protestant liberalism speaks frequently of man's greatness and brotherhood due to the Fatherhood of God. While seemingly
having a more distinctive religious framework than
secular philosophies that speak of man's greatness, it
too denies man's true reality by its excessive optimism
toward universal peace and goodwill. Liberalism,
therefore, has constantly fallen prey to the dangerous
practice of showing humanity its "greatness too
clearly, apart from his vileness." To the contrary,
more traditional and orthodox theologies have so
emphasized man's sinfulness and separation from God
that they have frequently left the individual man or
woman with feelings of absolute despair and worthless-
ness akin to the most pessimistic expressions of
existentialism. Biblical man, however, is both great
and wretched, both dignified and depraved. Our goal in
this chapter is to present this biblical picture of
man's true identity of created godlikeness and the
abnormal actuality of his total depravity.

Genesis 1:27 concisely states man's distinctive
creation:

43

> And God created man in His own
> image, in the image of God He
> created Him: male and female He
> created them.

Here is the source of man's dignity. Humans are
different from the rest of God's living creatures in
that they are made in the very image of God. Being
made in the image of God does not mean physical
likeness for we know God is spirit and not body (John
4:24). Genesis 5:1 helps us in that it tells us that
"when God created man, He made him in the likeness of
God." James 3:9 asks how we can use the same tongue to
bless God and "curse men, who have been made in the
likeness of God."[2] Image and likeness are thus
seemingly identical. John Calvin wrote that "as for
myself, before I define the image of God, I would deny
that it differs from his likeness."[3] Though God and
man are obviously greatly different in that God is
infinite and man finite, image and likeness certainly
convey that humans have a general resemblance or
similarity with God. It is this similarity with God,
given by God, that gives men and women their unique
dignity and places them at the pinnacle of God's
physical creation. This similarity with God is the
very basis and reason why capital punishment is
instituted against those who attack God's image by
murdering a man (Genesis 9:6). What then is this
similarity or resemblance between God's creatures and
Himself?

Genesis 1:28, which immediately follows the
statement that God created man in His image, seems to
connect this likeness with God's command to "subdue"
the earth and to "rule" over the other animate creations of God. In Genesis 2:19 the first step in this
subduing and ruling is seen by portraying God bringing
the animals to Adam "to see what he would call them,"
with the result that "whatever the man called a living
creature, that was its name." This ability to name the
animals reveals one aspect of God's image: man has a
rational verbal capacity.

Symbolic language is unique with humans. True,
animals signal one another of danger or desire to mate,
and some few may go beyond this, but no other creature
communicates in the breadth and depth of man. No other
animal has true language. One of the facts "of making
man in his own image," Francis Schaeffer notes, "is
that man is the verbalizer."[4] Man is the verbalizer

not only because of the gift of speaking itself, but because of man's capacity to symbolize and to think logically. Logic is at the very center of communication. Proper identifications, distinguishing things that differ, comparing two different objects by a third, presenting of evidence, shaping an hypothesis, tearing down or analysis of the parts or implications of an idea, are all various facets of logical rationality. This rationality absolutely separates mankind from the rest of creation. This rationality provides the very structure and possibility for both God's communication via special revelation to man as well as the human ability to respond to God and communicate with other individuals equally made in God's image. The first apparent use of this gift of language and logic is thus clearly seen when we read that all the animals and birds were brought to Adam to name them and whatever he "called a living creature, that was its name" (Genesis 2:19).

This ability to name the animals also demonstrates Adam's inherent, God-given, capacity for intellectual and artistic creativity. As God created everything out of nothing, so man reflects his divine image by creating names "out of nothing" for each creature. This finite creativity very definitely separates man from the rest of creation. Man's creativity is revealed in history in all of the arts. While all men are not equally artistic, all men do create. Though there are very few Picassos and Beethovens, there is creativity in every home demonstrated by the interior decorating of the parents, the attempt of adolescents at music composition, or smaller children by coloring on the walls!

Creativity, like rationality, may be used as depraved expressions of man's pride and selfishness rather than to God's glory and praise. Nevertheless, Christians cannot reject the full use of our minds in such areas as philosophy and science any more than we may deny the artistic gifts and accomplished expressions of either our own young people or the creative talents of newly saved individuals. The Bible records numerous instances of artistic creativity from the blueprint of the Tabernacle (Exodus 25:9-40) to the fruition of Solomon's temple and elaborate palace in 1 Kings 6:1-7:51. The plans for this beautiful temple David attributed to the Holy Spirit (1 Chronicles 28:11-19). This shows God's direct approval of the design and intricate art work of the Temple in the same way individual craftsmanship and refined skills were endorsed for the Tabernacle. Creative abilities and artistic talents are unique to man not only because of the God-given capacity of the divine image, but also because man alone is called to explicit worship of the Creator. From Bible times to the present, artistry has been and must continue to be understood as a worthy means to glorify God and aid our neighbor into an experience of God's grace. All art and creativity is obviously not for direct use in worship, but no art is legitimate for the believing Christian that is not compatible with the holiness of God. While art need not be the realistic copying of God's nature, neither can art so burst the structured parameters of creation that it denies all order and purposefulness. A biblical balance encourages creativity, even creativity for creativity's sake since we are unable to give absolute reasons why God Himself originally created. Nevertheless, biblical balance also means that the Christian community need not accept all art as the direct expression of God-given creativity. Much art needs to be evaluated and even negatively criticized as fallen man may and does pervert creativity for the sake of his own godlessness. Just as the architectural wonder at Babel was not the rightful use of man's gifts and talents but rather a monument to man's arrogance and pride, so much art, music, even rhetoric, is equally perverted and sinful expressions of fallen man's God-given abilities. This misuse of art and creativity by depraved individuals, however, may never be used as an excuse for the neglect and non-cultivation of creativity in the Christian community. If it is, biblical balance is also dismissed with the dismissal of creativity.

God's image is not totally identified by noting our verbal, rational, and creative gifts. Man is also inherently personal and thus capable of willful decision-making and moral responsibility. Man was made to commune personally with God, but also to be obedient to the infinite Creator as the finite creature. Genesis 2:16, 17 states both the awesome responsibility of decision-making but also the possibility of its dire consequences:

> And the LORD God commanded the man, saying, "From any tree of the garden you may eat freely; but from the tree of the knowledge of good and evil you shall not eat, for in

the day that you eat from it you
shall die" (Genesis 2:16, 17).

Adam not only understood this command, it was a
genuine imperative that could be either obeyed or
disobeyed. God neither made Adam that he could not
sin, nor that he had to sin. Man was free to obey or
disobey in his original state. We cannot doubt or
question why God made man so! Saint Augustine, while
rightly denying that man has a free will after the
initial disobedience and sin, also rightly dismissed
the false dilemma many have thought they perceived in
God creating Adam with a free choice of obedience or
disobedience. Augustine wrote that free will:

> is good and divinely given; and you
> should grant that those who make
> evil use of free will ought to be
> condemned rather than saying that
> He who gave it ought not to have
> given it.[5]

The wrong use of free will did condemn Adam and all his
posterity (Romans 5:12). The results, as Augustine
noted, were that men and women alike would approve
"false things as true" and lack the "power to abstain
from lust because of the opposition and torments of the
bondage of the flesh"--two things "not in the nature of
man as he was made," but "the penalties of man who has
been condemned." Therefore, "when we speak of the will
that is free to do right, we speak of the will with
which man was [first] made."[6]

This is why man is not simply dignified, but
depraved as well. But before looking at this dark side
of man as he now is, we must look a little closer at
Adam and Eve as they came from the Creator's hands.
Adam was first made, then Eve, as Paul states in
1 Timothy 2:13. But this simply signifies the order of
creation not inequality. Both were created in the same
image of God and are therefore absolutely equal as to
worth and possibilities of fellowship with God as well
as in their respective creative and rational capacities
and moral responsibility. Adam, however, did have God-
given responsibility for guidance and protection of his
wife because of the very order of creation which is
evidenced in his naming of her as "woman" (Genesis
2:23). Adam, then, is held responsible for the actual
disobedience as he did not fulfill his God-given
responsibility as husband. To Eve, the reiteration of

the divine order is plain in Genesis 3:16, though it must be remembered that the order is husband/wife, not man/woman. This biblical balance between male/female as to equality but a distinct order is restated in no uncertain terms in Galatians 3:28 and 1 Corinthians 11:3-16.

Personhood and moral responsibility are inherent in man and woman being created in God's image. No other creatures were made to have direct and explicit relationship with God. This personhood was created holy and righteous as a finite reflection of God. The relationship between creator/creature is obviously to be one of dependence and obedience of the creature to his Creator. But because of God's initial gift of free will through His image, the history of the God/human relationship has actually been a "conflict of wills." The temptation by Satan of Eve in Genesis 3:1-6 is nearly identical with all subsequent temptation. Mankind is always tempted to deny the Creator/creature distinction. Man desires to be "like God" absolutely rather than relativity. In our language of today, man desires "to do his own thing" rather than "to will God's will" in responsible stewardship of God's creation. Adam and Eve, and we, are deceived in denying the very character of God as we deny God's truthfulness in believing the devil's lie that "you surely shall not die" (Genesis 3:4). This denial of God's Word is the persistent practice of Satan, but the original pair believed the "father of lies" rather than the personification of Truth--God. We, like them, fall for Satan's denial of God's goodness, as if God selfishly attempts to keep something good and proper from us. Satan states: "For God knows that in the day you eat from it your eyes will be opened, and you will be like God, knowing good and evil" (Genesis 3:5). Once we believe God untrue, we fall for anything and even believe the infinite Creator's nature to be selfish and egocentric as if He were finite, indulgent, and less than absolutely holy. It is then a very short step to deny God's total "otherness" from the creature and actually think we can "be like God"--absolute and autonomous. Man has now used his will to be free of God rather than to freely be obedient to God's truthful, completely holy, and absolutely perfect will. Man is now "free of God" only to be in complete volitional bondage to Satan, self, and sin. Man is now separate from the very source of his being. He is estranged and in need of reconciliation to His Creator and intended Lord. In Scriptural terms, man is dead--separated from

48

God, his true created self, and others. The real possibility of <u>eternal</u> <u>separation</u> from God hangs over his head and is much more threatening and damning than even the fear of a mushroom cloud. In theological terms, man is totally depraved.

There is one remnant in man that reminds him intimately of his moral responsibility and intended obedience to the will of His Creator--conscience. Scripture, while not denying cultural and social influence on one's moral practices and resultant guilt, nevertheless implies that the conscience is more than one's education and upbringing. Webster defines conscience as "the sense or consciousness of the moral goodness or blameworthiness of one's own conduct, intentions, or character together with a feeling of obligation to do right or be good; a faculty, power, or principle enjoining good acts."[7] Conscience reflects one's response to the moral law that is written on our hearts because we are God's creations. Romans 2:14, 15 speaks of Gentiles, who while not having the law of Moses, nevertheless have the law of God written on their heart and therefore their conscience either accuses them of breaking the moral law or defends and excuses them because their deeds have been in accordance with "the Law written in their hearts." The Ten Commandments were given to clearly reveal moral evil and the sinfulness of disobeying the moral law (Romans 5:13, 20; 7:7-13). However, before the Ten Commandments, the men of the book of Genesis were not only held responsible for their moral waywardness as evidenced by Noah's flood and the destruction of Sodom and Gomorrah, but even the pagan Pharoah of Egypt knew the evil of having Abraham's wife when Abraham had said Sarai was his sister (Genesis 12:10-20). Abraham played the same trick on Abimelech, but because he had not yet touched Sarai, Abimelech claimed a "clear conscience" and God replies, "Yes, I know you did this with a clear conscience, and so I have kept you from sinning against me" (Genesis 20:5, 6, NIV). The point that must be emphasized is that both men knew a moral law prior to the Ten Commandments. By means of this innate moral law one knew guilt and punishment while the other had a clear conscience ("integrity of heart," NASV) because he had not sinned against God. This reveals the reality of sin before the written law and thus necessitates the existence of a moral law "written on the heart." Numerous other incidents could be appealed to in Genesis to establish the reality of man's apparently intuitive knowledge of God's moral expectations prior to the Mosaic Law.

Conscience, however, as the faculty that judges or excuses us of maintaining or breaking God's law, is not an absolutely reliable guide. As previously mentioned, conscience is at least in some degree conditioned by our moral and social environment. Cultures steeped in immoral practices will likely not collectively feel the judgment of conscience, though some individuals may feel guilty and question the morality of his society for particular practices. This questioning of societal practices, and more importantly the prior moral prescriptions in regard to the maintenance of life, sexual relations, personal property, truth-telling, etc. are presented by C. S. Lewis to show that such questioning and universality of moral restrictions not only differentiates man from everything else, but also demonstrates the existence of a universal moral law, a Tao, and thus the probability of a Lawgiver.[8] Nevertheless, Paul warns us that some men are so willfully sinful, and are so degraded, that they are "seared in their own conscience as with a branding iron" and "both their mind and their conscience are defiled" because "they have become callous, have given themselves over to sensuality, for the practice of every kind of impurity with greediness" (1 Timothy 4:2; Titus 1:15; Ephesians 4:19). This introduces us to the other side of man--depravity.[9]

Men and women as they actually exist are not only possessors of great dignity by being made in God's image, and of obvious worth as proven by the incarnation, but are also absolutely depraved, sinful, and separated from God. We have previously alluded to this depravity in man's perverted use of his creative abilities and rational capacities. We have looked briefly at the initial fall of man which mirrors man's constant denial of God's truthfulness, goodness, and "otherness" in our perverted perspective and depraved nature in separation from God. Man, in short, is spiritually dead! His conscience is unreliable regardless of the reality of the moral law and God Himself being stamped on his inner psyche. "For even though they knew God, they did not honor Him as God, or give thanks; but they became futile in their speculations, and their foolish heart was darkened" (Romans 1:21).

This chapter is not completely balanced as to space devoted to man's dignity and depravity. This is not because of the writer's predisposition in emphasizing the former, but rather that we evangelical and fundamental Christians frequently only emphasize the latter. Thus the scales need balanced in remembering who we are originally and to Whom we are ultimately related. On the other hand, there must be no attenuation of who we actually are, sinners--separated from God. Even if this is an abnormal condition and not what God intended us to be, but what we chose to be, we are nevertheless fools while pretending to be wise since we have "exchanged the truth of God for a lie, and worshipped and served the creature rather than the Creator" (Romans 1:25).

Total depravity is frequently misunderstood by conservatives and liberals alike. Total depravity does not mean that every individual is as thoroughly sinful as he might be nor that depraved man cannot perform actions that are good in the sight of man. It does not mean that man is insignificant and meaningless because the very fact of the incarnation demonstrates not only God's love, but man and nature's inherent value and worth. But equally unbalanced is the denial of man's sinfulness and depravity that eliminates the Cross as old-fashioned superstition. Instead the Incarnation, Crucifixion, Resurrection vividly announce and demonstrate both the essential dignity and total depravity of man. Lewis Sperry Chafer correctly notes that depravity is not man's estimation of himself, but God's estimation. He writes:

> If, as viewed by man, it is asserted that there is nothing good in man, the statement is untrue; for, as man is quick to declare, there is no human being so degraded that there is not some good in him. If, on the other hand, as viewed by God, it is claimed that man is without merit in His sight, the case is far different. Depravity as a doctrine does not stand or fall on the ground of man's estimation of himself; it rather reflects God's estimation of man.10

What then is God's estimation of man? Jeremiah 17:9 states that man's "heart is more deceitful than

51

all else and is desperately sick; who can understand it?" Before the flood, and it is safe to say afterward as well as far as humanity in general is concerned, we read that "the Lord saw that the wickedness of man was great on the earth, and that every intent of the thoughts of his heart was only evil continually" (Genesis 6:5). This estimation of man's bent away from God toward self and sinfulness is what the theologian means when he speaks of the total depravity of man. In other words, total depravity means the total absence of holiness and original righteousness if not, as noted above, the greatest intensity of sin. But depravity does not only describe the abnormal corruption of man's character and nature after the Fall, but also that there is nothing in man that can commend him to a holy and righteous God. Man has no spiritual good, nor can he earn any such good or merit in relation to God. Isaiah 64:6-7 says:

> For all of us have become like one
> who is unclean,
> And all our righteous deeds are
> like a filthy garment;
> And all of us wither like a leaf,
> And our iniquities, like the wind,
> take us away.
> And there is no one who calls on
> Thy name,
> Who arouses himself to take hold of
> Thee;
> For Thou has hidden Thy face from
> us,
> And hast delivered us into the
> power of our iniquities.

This passage is specifically addressed to the nation of Judah in their apostasy, but it may also be justly applied to man in general. Similarly Isaiah 53:6 says "all of us like sheep have gone astray, each of us has turned to his own way, but the LORD has caused the iniquity of us all to fall on Him." Every man is separated from God by inherent inclination from birth. Romans 5:12, 14 asserts that death and separation "spread to all men, because all sinned" in Adam since "death reigned from Adam until Moses, even over those who had not sinned in the likeness of the offense of Adam." (That is, they had not broken a definite command of God like Adam in the garden, and could not until the Ten Commandments were given, but nevertheless they died as sinners because they had "sinned" in and with Adam in his sin, and they had personally broken the law written on their heart as God's creatures.) All men are thus damned by their own sinful actions that distinctly express our essence and state. Man cannot approach God in his present, if abnormal, state. Righteousness is required if we are to be reunited with God and have the normal fellowship and relationship with the One in Whose image we were originally made. Man was created as righteous personhood. This is our normal or expected state. Our inherited condition as unrighteous or depraved personhood must be changed if communion with God is to be resumed. Only God can change us to be capable and desirous of such a reunion. Total depravity makes such a change inherently impossible from man's side. But Christ has both "redeemed us from the curse of the Law, having become a curse for us" and made possible a restored righteousness by becoming "sin on our behalf, that we might become the righteousness of God in Him" (Galatians 3:13; 2 Corinthians 5:21).

As believers we must remember that we too were totally depraved. Though we have a restored righteousness through Christ and therefore a restored relationship, it is not due to our intrinsic merit or greater goodness that God has been so gracious to us. While we have heard and answered the Gospel proclamation and call, the new creation in which old things have passed away and "new things have come" (2 Corinthians 5:17) is totally the work of the Holy Spirit. The Spirit's original regeneration and continuous molding work is for the purpose of us being a "new self who is being renewed to a true knowledge according to the image of the One who created us" (Colossians 3:10). Paul reminds us, however, in 1 Corinthians 6:9-11 that the believers of Corinth as well as ourselves may have practiced the most terrible sins before we were washed, sanctified, and justified "in the name of the Lord Jesus Chist, and in the Spirit of our God." Similarly, Titus is reminded that both he and Paul himself "also once were foolish" as well as "disobedient, deceived, enslaved, to various lusts and pleasures, spending our life in malice and envy, hateful, hating one another" (Titus 3:3).[11] This state of alienation and absolute autonomy from God is changed only because of the abundant grace, unlimited love, and infinite saving power of the holy and truthful God.

Man, then, is both dignified and depraved! This is the biblical picture of man. Dignity and depravity are characteristics of man even as spirit and nature are distinguishable qualities of man and not separate parts (Genesis 2:7). Man is a whole and we cannot separate his depravity from his dignity any more than we can separate man's spirit from his body and still have man.[12] A balanced picture of man means we must stress both man's created dignity and self-acquired depravity. Christianity cannot be Christianity with an emphasis only on man's greatness that essentially denies our fallenness because there would then be no need of the incarnation, thus no Jesus, the Christ, and thus no Christianity. But at the same time, a Christianity that functionally only affirms the sinful wretchedness of ourselves obviously can proclaim the heart of Christianity in the incarnate, crucified, and resurrected Savior we so desperately need, but nevertheless will have difficulty in answering why God did so much for us, and why all avenues of legitimate vocations are open to us as the earth's divinely appointed steward. This latter perspective may be a Christianity of sorts, but it is not a Christianity truly reflecting and echoing biblical balance. Pascal, with whom we began, is correct! It is "dangerous to leave men in ignorance of both" their greatness and their vileness. "But it is very advantageous to show him both," for while we are neither brutes nor angels, it is absolutely necessary for us to know "both sides" of our nature if we are to be both realistic and biblical.[13] Though David may assert that man is "a little lower than God" (Psalm 8:5), Isaiah also says, "I am ruined! Because I am a man of unclean lips, and I live among a people of unclean lips; for my eyes have seen the King, the LORD of hosts" (Isaiah 6:5). Paul, however, also affirms hope in his rhetorical question and answer: "Wretched man that I am! Who will set me free from the body of this death? Thanks be to God through Jesus Christ our Lord!" (Romans 7:24, 25a). These three statements must each be affirmed by biblical Christianity. This alone is biblical balance in regard to ourselves.

REFLECTION

1. Discuss the possible heresy of either liberal or conservative Christianity in regard to man.

2. What does it mean to be made in the "likeness of God" (Genesis 5:1; James 3:9). Why is some dimension of similarity between God and man necessary for their communicative relationship?

3. List various facets of what it means to be created "in the image of God" (Genesis 1:27). Discuss the importance of reason and creativity in particular. What do these gifts of God imply for Christian education?

4. What is the significance of Genesis 2:16, 17 for Christian ethics? Identify the objective content and basis of a universal ethic. To what degree is the conscience normative for ethical decision-making?

5. Identify the biblical perspective to the relationship between male and female. Interpret Galatians 3:28 and 1 Corinthians 11:3-16 in the context of Genesis 1:26; 2:23; 3:16.

6. Discuss Genesis 3:1-6. How is the Fall of humanity in Adam and Eve a model of all temptation situations and our individual experiences of falling prey to sin? Compare this passage with our Lord's experience of temptation recorded in Matthew 4:1-11. Explain how Christ successfully meets the same threefold temptation.

7. Define total depravity. What is meant by original sin in light of Romans 5:12? Is there any hope of man pleasing God or meriting His favor in this condition? If not, summarize the biblical solution. Why, then, must each of the following verses be affirmed for a biblically balanced doctrine of man: Psalm 8:5; Isaiah 6:5; Romans 7:24, 25a?

[1]Blaise Pascal, The Thoughts of Blaise Pascal, edited by Brunschvicg (Garden City, New York: Doubleday, n.d.), no. 418.

[2]It is interesting to note that the Greek word homoiosis that is used of man being made in God's likeness in James 3:9 is the same word used of Christ "being made in the likeness of men" in Philippians 2:7. As we saw in the previous chapter, this word means that Christ was similar if not identical with fallen man. Thus when used in James it definitely conveys the essential similarity between God and man, though not their identity as God is infinite and man is finite.

[3]John Calvin, Calvin's Commentaries, The Pentateuch (Grand Rapids: AP&P Publishers, n.d.), I, 10.

[4]Francis Schaeffer, He Is There And He Is Not Silent (Wheaton, Illinois: Tyndale House Publishers, 1972), p. 65.

[5]Augustine, On Free Choice of the Will, translated by Anna S. Benjamin and L. H. Hackstaff (Indianapolis: Bobbs-Merrill, 1964), II, 18.

[6]Ibid., III, 18.

[7]Webster's New Collegiate Dictionary (Springfield, Massachusetts: G. & C. Merriam Company, 1973), p. 240.

[8]C. S. Lewis, Abolition of Man (New York: Macmillan, 1961).

[9]While we were not necessarily as evil and immoral as we might have been before salvation, every person's conscience is insufficient due to the depravity of man prior to regeneration. Hebrews 10:22 pictures this change as drawing "near with a sincere heart in full assurance of faith, having our hearts sprinkled clean from an evil conscience. . . ." Even salvation, however, will not guarantee that our conscience is an adequate voice apart from the Holy Spirit, Scripture, and prayer.

[10]Lewis Sperry Chafer, Systematic Theology (Dallas: Dallas Seminary Press, 1964), II, 218-219.

[11]Note also Ephesians 4:17, 18 which plainly instructs us that we "walk no longer just as the Gentiles also walk, in the futility of their mind, being darkened in their understanding, excluded from the life of God, because of the ignorance that is in them, because of the hardness of their heart." Believers thus have new life based on new knowledge of the Gospel. Unbelievers have no new life because their mind is vain or useless, it is "in the dark," willfully ignorant of God because of the very hardness of their heart, or in other words, the very depravity of their being.

[12]"The Hebrew conceived of man as an animated body and not as an incarnate soul." H. Wheeler Robinson, Inspiration and Revelation in the Old Testament (Oxford: Oxford University Press, 1946), p. 70.

[13]Pascal, loc. cit.

CHAPTER VI

GENERAL REVELATION--BOTH WITHIN AND WITHOUT

In chapter one we identified two realities: God and creation. Within the created realm we again found two dimensions, spirit and nature. Created nature is physical and/or material. Christianity must resist the tendency we noted earlier of having only half-the-pie by playing down the importance of nature and the physical aspects of life. This is especially true in regard to man himself who <u>alone</u> is both nature and spirit by being made in the image of God as well as from the dust of the ground (Genesis 1:26; 2:7). Man thus uniquely participates in <u>both</u> dimensions of the created realm--spirit and nature.

We also saw in chapter one, as Paul experienced in Athens (Acts 17:18-31), that human speculation and philosophy attempt to understand man as either totally physical and material (e.g. Epicureans believed that individuals were simply a collection of atoms that completely dissipate at death) or as entirely spirit and quite likely pantheistic (e.g. Stoicism). Paul realized that both the Epicureans and the Stoics were partially correct, but ultimately completely in error. Man is more than the dust of the ground as God created man distinctly in His image so as to have personal relationship with him. The stamp of "God-made" is obvious to every man as he contemplates his own nature and character. Man is inherently religious <u>because</u> he was made to have fellowship and relationship with the personal God. This is why the Athenians were "very religious" (Acts 17:22). The excessiveness of Athenian religiosity is shown by their idol "to an unknown God" (Acts 17:23). Theirs was a "catholic paganism." This religiosity was the very means of Paul's approach to the non-theistic philosophers of the Athenian Areopagus where idols of gold, silver, and stone abounded.

Paul, then, used this idol "to an unknown god" as an open door for evangelism among these ancient philosophers who were ignorant of the Old Testament. He could not argue and reason "with them from the Scriptures" as he had at his previous stops in the synagogues of Thessalonica and Berea as well as Athens (Acts 17:1, 2, 10, 11, 16, 17; see also 18:4, 19; 19:8). The philosophers neither knew nor accepted as authoritative God's special revelation of Himself in deed and word as recorded in the Old Testament. Rather

Paul had to appeal to the general revelation of God in nature and man that is universal, in no need of translation (Psalm 19:1-3), and of which no one can claim ignorance. The God of creation is the God of general revelation. It is this God, the particularly "unknown" but "generally known" God, that Paul announces to the philosophers and general populace of Athens--"what therefore you worship in ignorance, this I proclaim to you" (Acts 17:23).

Paul's ensuing argument has two prongs: the omnipotent and independence of the Creator God, and the necessary Personhood of God if we are His "offsprings." The "unknown God" Paul introduces to the Athenian philosophers is the God of the Genesis account of creation, but he does not quote or in any way directly appeal to the Old Testament as authoritative, though it most certainly is such for himself. Rather Paul appeals to "the God who made the world and all things in it" (vs. 24). To a Jewish audience this would have been an explicit reference to the Old Testament; but to Paul's Gentile and pagan audience the explicit appeal is to the presence of undeniable reality and the question of its original source! Paul is not simply a philosopher here arguing for a First Cause. Rather Paul is arguing on the basis of man's common sense and intuitive awareness that the "world and all things in it" are not self-caused nor eternal. Man cannot escape the fact that he is God's creature, made in God's image, simply on intellectual grounds. No the witness of one's own being, his _ontos_, or in other terms, his _psyche_ demands such.

This being the case, is it reasonable to believe that the Creator of everything could be "housed" in man-made buildings, or that He needed gifts from man since He alone "gives to all life and breath and all things" (vs. 25)? The gods of the Parthenon were limited. While he does not say it, they were actually the products of man's imagination and myth-making propensities which reflect man's inherent religiosity every bit as much as the idol "to an unknown God." The God Whom he is introducing, however, is the "Lord of heaven and earth," completely self-sufficient and totally absolute! This "unknown God" is not the god of a specific geographical region nor is He limited to a particular people. Rather He is the One Who constructed the various boundaries of the numerous ethnic differences of man, having made the many from the one-- Adam (vs. 26).

This presentation before the Athenian court is totally compatible with Paul's statement concerning general revelation in Romans 1:18-20:

> For the wrath of God is revealed from heaven against all ungodliness and unrighteousness of men, who suppress the truth in unrighteousness, because that which is known about God is evident within them; for God made it evident to them. For since the creation of the world His invisible attributes, His eternal power and divine nature, have been clearly seen, being understood through what has been made, so that they are without excuse.

Verse 20 is the theoretical statement of Paul's actual practice in Athens. From the moment of creation so-to-speak, "the God who made the world and all things in it" (Acts 17:24) has been mediately known "through what has been made" (Romansn 1:20). This does not imply that God is either personally or exhaustively known through the visible facets of creation. Nevertheless, the existence of an all-powerful, totally good Being, is existentially demanded by the scope, nature, and quality of the physical reality which undubitably indicates God's reality and invisible attributes. General revelation is simply the obverse side of creation. Given creation, the reality of God must be seen. As a finished canvas portends an artist as well as implicitly saying something about his or her person, so creation intuitively "points" to the grandeur and infinity of God.

Paul's Roman statement also agrees with the other "prong" of his speech before the philosophers--"For we also are His offspring" (Acts 17:28). In Romans 1:19 he writes that "that which is known about God is evident _within_ them" [italics added]. Thus man cannot avoid the witness of general revelation as he himself is an expression of it. John Calvin wrote that "all men of sound judgment will therefore hold that a sense of Deity is indelibly engraven on the human heart."[1] Paul graphically portrays this fact by men groping in the dark, or as a blind man, in their attempt to find God (Acts 17:28). This groping is intuitive but inadequate. Humans are inherently religious as the Athenians demonstrated in their profuse religiosity, but they will not find the holy Creator by such misdirected and uncertain searching. Nevertheless, it is true that "in Him we live and move and exist" (Acts 17:28) as even the pagan poets seemingly realized. The quotation Paul used was originally no doubt understood pantheistically, but Paul can carefully use it to express the biblical conception of God as well since we do exist only in His willing grace and mercy, if not corporately within Him. We are His "offspring"! That is, we are made in God's image. Greeks, as well as the Hebrews, logically knew that the personal could not derive from, or be created by, the impersonal. Thus if man is personal, then God could not be impersonal. This is the heart-and-soul of Paul's argument when he states that "being then the offspring of God, we ought not to think that the Divine Nature is like gold or silver or stone, an image formed by the art and thought of man" (Acts 17:29).

This is a very important argument Paul makes here. First, it assumes the validity of the laws of logic. That is, man cannot be personal if God is impersonal and we humans are His offspring. Like comes from like. Pesonal beings do not derive their personality from impersonal objects, not even costly ones like gold or silver. Rather, as an Epicurean son resembles his Epicurean philosopher father, we resemble God as "His offspring" by being personal beings even as He. Thus, secondly, the gods of the Parthenon are insufficient to explain the character of our own existence. The God Paul is introducing is uniquely Personal. This is the essential "trait" that necessitates that the knowledge of God is within us in the Romans statement. Man was and is made to have personal fellowship with the Person/Creator. This is why Augustine correctly wrote that "Thou hast formed us for Thyself, and our hearts are restless till they find rest in Thee."2

There remains yet two aspects in regard to general revelation we must note--its denial by humanity and its results for humanity. Verse 18 states that God's wrath is upon all ungodliness and unrighteousness. Adam and us are ungodly before we are unrighteous. The word translated "ungodliness" means a "positive and active irreligion" and is "contemplated as a deliberate withholding from God of his dues of prayer and of service, a standing, so to speak, in battle array against Him."3 It is Adam and Eve denying God's absolute uniqueness and "otherness" in falling for Satan's deceptive temptation that "you will be like God, knowing good and evil" (Genesis 3:5). It is no different for us. We are born separated and alienated from God. Thus in full "battle array" of ungodliness we commit deeds and thoughts of unrighteousness, or sins, against both God and other men.[4] Our humanity, then, is both a religious and a moral failure. Nevertheless, we and the original pair bare the stamp of God's image and thus "hold the truth in unrighteousness" (KJV).

There is some debate, evidenced by the differences in English translations, whether we "hold" or "hold down" the "truth in unrighteousness." Greek experts are aligned on both sides. It seems that only the context determines whether the original word is to be translated as "hold," meaning "possess," or as "hold down," meaning to "suppress."[5] The King James and the New American Standard versions, as can be seen in the above quotations, are not agreed. The difficulty amounts to the lack of a contextual indication of Paul's precise meaning. Lacking such, either transla- tion is feasible. This, however, is most likely exactly what Paul desires to express. Humans "hold" or "possess" the truth of God's reality inherently in their individual spirit, psyche, and conscience (cf. Romans 2:14, 15 and chapter 5 above). This is the way in which they were created. They cannot escape such "intuitive" revelation. At the same time, they "hold down" or "suppress" this revelation in their sinfulness and depravity so as to continue their charade of ultimate independence and self-sufficiency. Griffith Thomas notes this double meaning when he writes that the word in question "suggests that they possess the truth and suppress it by their unrighteous living"[6] [original italics]. Francis Schaeffer, in a more apologetic and philosophical manner, concludes the same when he writes that men:

> hold a portion of the truth, but they hold it in unrighteousness. They must hold some of the truth about themselves and the universe for they must live in the universe as God made it, but they refuse to carry these truths to their reasonable conclusions, because, whether they live in the ancient world or in the modern world, they

63

adhere to their false presuppo-
sitions.7

The combined force of general revelation's
universality and intrinsicalness is sufficient to leave
us "without excuse." While natural revelation without
man is general, it is nevertheless for all men as it
has no need for translation for "there is no speech or
language where [its] voice is not heard" (Psalm 19:1).
Every bit as universal, and considerably more ines-
capable, is the revelation of God within man. This
intrinsic sense of Deity, which Calvin remarks is
"beyond dispute," is given by God Himself "to prevent
any man from pretending ignorance."8 Man is sur-
rounded by general revelation both in and out. While
man may consciously or unconsciously suppress this
revelation of God, it does not alleviate his responsibility before a holy and personal God. Paul is
claiming in Romans what he practices at the Athenian
Court. Men may suppress the truth that surrounds him
of what is in regard to the nature of both the external
universe and himself, but he is "without excuse" in so
doing. The result of general revelation leaves every
single individual guilty before God. No one can plead
either innocence or ignorance. Every man is aware of
the reality of God both from outside of himself in the
existence of the natural universe and from inside
himself so that we are "condemned by [our] own conscience when [we] neither worship him nor consecrate
[our] lives to his service."9

Before returning to Paul's speech on the Areopagus, we must note that general revelation is never
sufficient in its own right to bring individuals to a
truly adequate knowledge of, and personal relationship
with, God. Even prior to the Fall, God provided Adam
and Eve with distinctive vocational and moral instructions that might be labeled special revelation (Genesis
1:28-30; 2:16, 17). General revelation is inherently
limited. It reveals only the existence of a divine
nature or divinity and this One's eternal power. In
Athens Paul also established through logical inference
the necessity of God's Personhood in light of our
personalness. But as sinners in particular we are in
need of specific revelation that reconciles us to God
and is not as easily distorted because of our post-fall
predisposition against God which causes us to suppress
the knowledge of God from general revelation. Men,
therefore, cannot get to the true God by means of
general revelation, not because there is something

wrong with God's revelation, but because there is something wrong with our moral inclinations and the perspective from which, and the way in which, we direct our reasoning abilities. A different perspective and a more submissive spirit is needed on our behalf as well as more specific revelation on God's behalf that culminates with His own enfleshment. As Calvin remarks, "Scripture, gathering together the impressions of Deity, which, till then, lay confused in their minds, dissipates the darkness, and shows us the true God clearly." Therefore, "it is necessary to apply to Scripture, in order to learn the sure marks which distinguish God, as the Creator of the world, from the whole herd of fictitious gods."[10]

This is precisely what Paul does at Athens. After he distinguishes God from the fictitious gods of the Areopagus by the two-fold argument from creation without and personalness within, Paul moves directly to the necessity of repentance in light of the coming judgment which will be administered by the acme of special revelation--God Himself in the Person of Jesus, the Christ. The final proof of this God's reality as well as the certainty of His plans has been furnished "to all men by raising Him [Jesus, the Christ] from the dead" (Acts 17:31). This claim brought immediate laughter to the naturalistic Epicureans and the deterministic Stoics. Resurrection was completely unintelligible from either world-view. Paul did not and could not retreat from the very essence of the gospel because of the unbiblical orientation of the individuals within his audience. It had been this emphasis of "Jesus and the resurrection" (vs. 18) that had prompted the original questions and thereby this opportunity to present the gospel to the intellectual elite of Athens. Regardless of the difficulty of comprehending such from their original perspective, the incipient truth of general revelation did prey on some minds who desired to hear him "again concerning this" (vs. 32). Others responded in belief to the truth of God's special revelation in and through Christ. Paul has thus used the general revelation that is both outside and inside man as it is intended and must be used--as a foundation and preparation for special revelation.

REFLECTION

1. Why are men inherently religious? Illustrate this from the source of secular philosophy--Athens. How does Paul use this fact to his advantage for the sake of Christian evangelism?

2. What is general revelation? Is there any difference between natural revelation and natural theology? If there is, explain the difference.

3. Identify the two parts of Paul's argument based on general revelation in Acts 17. Is his practice compatible with his theory in Romans 1? Explain.

4. Which of the two facets of general revelation do you believe is more telling upon unbelief? Why?

5. Define "ungodliness" and "unrighteousness." What is the relationship between these in Romans 1:18? Relate these concepts to the Fall and our own experiences of temptation.

6. Why is there ambiguity as to the interpretation of Romans 1:18b? Which interpretation do you favor? Is it possible that Paul really intends to claim that fallen men both possess and suppress the truth of general revelation? If it is, why is this the case?

7. Is it true that general revelation is inherently limited? If it is, how is it possible that mankind is left "without excuse" before God on the basis of general revelation?

ENDNOTES

[1] John Calvin, _Institutes of the Christian Religion_, trans. Henry Beveridge (Grand Rapids: William B. Eerdmans Publishing Company, 1964), I, 3, 3.

[2] Augustine, _Confessions_, trans. J. G. Pilkington (New York: Liveright Publishing Corporation, 1943), I, 1, 1.

[3] Richard Chenevix Trench, _Synonyms of the New Testament_ (Grand Rapids: William B. Eerdmans Publishing Company, 1953), p. 242.

[4] Ungodliness most likely refers to the first table of the Law and unrighteousness relates to the second table of the Law. This distinction between ungodliness and unrighteousness is maintained in the remainder of the chapter as Paul first addresses pagan impiety in verses 21-25 and their gross immorality in verses 26-32.

[5] Passages like 1 Corinthians 7:30 imply a positive "holding," but another passage such as 2 Thessalonoians 2:6, 7 certainly renders this word negatively as "restrain" or "suppress."

[6] W. H. Griffith Thomas, _St. Paul's Epistle to the Romans_ (Grand Rapids: William B. Eerdmans Publishing Company, 1946), p. 67.

[7] Francis Schaeffer, _Death in the City_ (Downers Grove, Illinois: Inter-Varsity Press, 1969), p. 102.

[8] Calvin, _op. cit._, I, 3, 1.

[9] _Ibid._

[10] _Ibid._, I, 6, 1.

CHAPTER VII

SPECIAL REVELATION: BOTH EVENT AND WORD

Revelation may be defined biblically as simply the "disclosure of truth." The New Testament word most often translated reveal comes from a compound word (apokalupto) that means "to uncover." Special revelation, unlike general revelation, is verbal and specific. Special revelation, understood Christianly, originates with God and is therefore largely dependent on supernatural agencies and means such as the Holy Spirit's inspiration of the Bible which is taken up in the following chapter.

There are two assumptions which make the possibility of special revelation highly probable, but which are not definitely known without that revelation. These are the existence of a personal, all-knowing and all-powerful God Who desires to communicate, and creatures who are other than God but are endowed with the capacity to logically and verbally receive such revelation. General revelation via the world around us and our own constitution witnesses to the reality of both of these assumptions. However, it is the actuality of this specific revelation of God's Person and Will and our intellectual comprehension of such that substantiates the validity of our assumptions. This chicken-and-egg problem cannot be eliminated in Christian doctrine for obviously there must be a God to have revelation of and from Him, but we will not have exact and definite knowledge of God and His purposes until the special revelation is received.

In recent years, even among Christians who definitely believe in the fact of special revelation, there has been much debate as to the nature of that revelation. Traditionally, Christianity has understood special revelation to be the Bible. This meant that special revelation was distinct verbal propositions that could not be discovered by natural means such as reason. It also meant that special revelation was frequently seen as solely verbal and therefore dogmatic propositions that could be intellectually accepted but existentially and practically forgotten. Such religion was frequently labeled "cold orthodoxy," be it Roman Catholic or Protestant.

To counteract this supposed wooden approach to revelation, various theologians began to speak and write of revelation as the self-manifestation of God. By this they meant that God's revelation cannot be reduced to verbal propositions, but rather is the meeting of Person with person. What is revealed is not propositions or statements about God, but God Himself. He unveils Himself by sharing Himself in a personal and existential manner with us. It is the encounter or confrontation of the finite subject before the infinite Subject. Many rivulets have contributed to this stream of thought, most notably Soren Kierkegaard (1813-1855), Martin Buber (1878-1965) and Karl Barth (1886-1968). This emphasis on encounter, however, went to the opposite extreme of "cold orthodoxy." Instead of knowledge with no personal relationship, Martin Buber, for instance, had relationship in his I-Thou encounter, but no knowledge! For, as Buber writes, "whoever says Thou does not have something; he has nothing. But he stands in relation."1

A personal understanding of divine revelation is indispensable. But the movement known as neo-orthodoxy, or sundry other names, tends to confuse the doctrine of illumination (the Holy Spirit's guidance to the truth, existential meaning, and personal acceptance of revelation, 2 Corinthians 2:14) with revelation itself. It is true that there is a sense in which the objective revelation of God is not in actuality revelation "for me" unless I respond to it and adopt it as God's provision and norms for my life. But if I fail to do this, it does not mean that there is no longer any objective, divine revelation. It simply means I personally do not have daily divine instruction and guidance, but God's revelation of Himself and his moral instructions for my lifestyle still objectively exist. In other words, there can be no revelation "for me," no believing in, without a revelation that is real, objective, and normative, providing content in which I may believe that about God. In other words, for me to believe in God, I must believe that God exists, "for he who comes to God must believe that He is" (Hebrews 11:6). Thus a faithful response to God's revelation must not only enable one to speak of a relationship, but as the character and will of a friend is known in a friendship, so one knows something about God that can be stated in true verbal propositions or one has no relationship and, even worse, no God. It is a mistake to think that orthodoxy, regardless of its poor implementation and/or practice at times, taught or believed that the content and object of faith was verbal statements about God rather than God Himself.

Rather the object of belief was always to be the reality which the propositions were thought to express and not the propositions themselves.

Special revelation initially took place in the garden prior to the Fall of Adam and Eve when they received the explicit command in regard to the tree of the knowledge of good and evil (Genesis 2:16, 17) and the seemingly continuous revelation of God as He would meet them daily (Genesis 3:8). Special revelation is thus initiated in the divine love and grace of God on behalf of His creatures. This is particularly seen when, post-Fall, special revelation takes on the primary task of delineating God's redemptive plans and purposes. This can be seen immediately in Genesis 3:15 and 4:3-7, but it is throughout the Scriptures, culminating in the statement in regard to Christ in Hebrews 1:1, 2 to which we shall return. Special revelation is understood in this chapter, then, as the demonstration and sharing by God of His Person, Will, and redemptive activity. As such, special revelation is both the self-manifestation of God personally, as well as His redemptive acts in history that are susceptible to historical investigation, and the verbal propositions of the Bible that provide us both true assertions of God's being and nature and absolutely accurate interpretations of the significance of His historical activity. God acts redemptively in history as seen in Israel's temporal deliverance in the Old Testament, and ours and their eternal salvation through the death and resurrection of the truly historical and incarnate Son of God, Jesus of Nazareth.

Special revelation is not the logical necessity, or flip-side, of creation as general revelation is. Rather it is the story of God's gracious provision for man's self-induced but catastrophic plight in total alienation and separation from Himself. Special revelation is primarily for fallen man (the Garden excepted) and is therefore remedial and redemptive. While general revelation comes to all men simply because they are God's creatures living in God's universe, special revelation is provided to and for man as sinners. Special revelation, however, does not supersede the general revelation given to man as man, but supplements it in light of the new condition of man and the broken fellowship between God and man.

In addition to man's sinful plight that evokes God's remedial revelation, there is the absolute transcendence of the infinite God. The transcendence of God simply means that He is "beyond," "other than," everything else. Man <u>cannot</u> reach or definitively and personally know God by either empirical inferences from the world around him, or by rationalistic deductions of intellectual or moral arguments for God's existence. Even if we were able to correctly infer the existence of the infinite from the finite (a logical impossibility), it would be insufficient in itself, for the demons know of God's existence (James 2:19) but did not, do not, and will not accord Him the proper reverence and worship due to His Name.[2]

Because of God's transcendence and infinity, all revelation of His Person and Will must be by means of divine condescension. Special revelation is a mediated revelation. It is cosmic. That is it must take on the forms of this world. It is also anthropomorphic. God makes Himself accessible by uncovering Himself in terms of mankind. This is of course possible because man was and is still made in the image of God. Just as the acme of revelation, the incarnation, is possible because of man being in God's image, so all personal uncovering of God in special revelation is also feasible because of this same fact. John Calvin refers to this condescension of Scripture as accommodating "the knowledge of him to our feebleness" when it reveals God in terms of a "mouth, ears, eyes, hands and feet." God, in so speaking to us, "lisps with us as nurses are wont to do with little children."[3] Special revelation, in short, respects man's creaturely existence, adjusts to it, and mediates itself by it to the consciousness of man.

Special revelation is thus the necessary and supernatural projection of God into the domain of human history that makes a profound difference for that particular era as well as providing distinct evidence of God's character and faithfulness for all generations. This is quite clearly seen in the history of Israel. From Abraham on, the nation of Israel was the recipient of God's revelatory/redemptive activity that distinguished her from among the nations. From the plagues, especially the Passover, through the crossing of the Sea of Reeds to the institution of the sacrificial system, God was progressively revealing both His Person and Will through His redemptive program. The plagues, for instance, gave both the pagan Egyptians and the faint-hearted Jews evidence of God's reality and protective provision for His people (Exodus 7:3-5).

The Israelite crossing of the Sea of Reeds, and the Egyptian calamity, were predicted and interpreted by Moses:

> "Do not fear! Stand by and see the salvation of the Lord which He will accomplish for you today; for the Egyptians whom you have seen today, you will never see them again forever." . . . And when Israel saw the great power which the Lord had used against the Egyptians, the people feared the Lord, and they believed in the Lord and in His servant Moses (Exodus 14:13, 31).

The difference between ordinary historical events and extraordinary historical events such as the above are their supernatural character and revelatory function. Special revelation is inherently supernatural. This is necessarily the case whenever God's self-disclosure and activity intervene in history. These were the miraculous but historical events that the Jews were told by Moses to remember throughout their history so that they might trust in the Lord their God (Deuteronomy 4:9, 34; 7:17-19). This is exactly what Joshua did after possessing the land. In Joshua 24 he calls all the tribes to Shechem and rehearses their God-provided and God-protected history, beginning with Abraham. This relationship between God's revelatory activity and their trustful allegiance and service is clearly stated by the people in verses 16-18:

> "Far be it from us that we should forsake the Lord to serve other gods; for the Lord our God is He who brought us and our fathers up out of the land of Egypt, from the house of bondage, and who did these great signs in our sight and preserved us through all the ways in which we went and among all the peoples through whose midst we passed. And the Lord drove out from before us all the peoples, even the Amorites who lived in the land. We also will serve the Lord, for He is our God."

73

This was not simply a first-generation, post-Moses, experience. The people of God realized that their victories and their judgments were the direct or indirect activity of the Lord their God. Numerous Psalms, such as Psalm 105 recited by David in 1 Chronicles 16, keep the God-interpreted events before Israelite hearts and minds. David desires to "make known among the nations what he has done. Sing to him, sing praise to him; tell of all his wonderful acts" (1 Chronicles 16:8, 9 which is also Psalm 105:1, 2). David continues: "Declare his glory among the nations, his marvelous deeds among all peoples." "For all the gods of the nations are idols, but the Lord made the heavens" (1 Chronicles 16:24, 26 and Psalm 96:3, 5). Jehoshaphat, like Hezekiah later, recognized God's revelatory involvement in his nation's history (2 Chronicles 20:5-12). Thus many events of Israelite history are the ingredients of special revelation that distinguishes the true God from all the false idols. Elijah knew this well in his encounter with the priests of Baal (1 Kings 18:20-39, especially verses 36, 37). As Elijah stated, "the God who answers by fire, He is God" (1 Kings 18:24). He Who is the "living God" is the "true God" (Jeremiah 10:10). The idols may be stone, but God is acting in history and reveals himself as not only the true, but the only living God!

Historical events are open and liable to various and diverse interpretations. Revelation as historical event, therefore, is in need of revelation as Word, and in the case of prophecy, vice versa. In fact, the very declaration of God's Word and its coming to pass was the express test of distinguishing between true and false prophets in Israel (Deuteronomy 18:22; Jeremiah 28:1-17). God thus provides His revelation in history with an absolute and definite interpretation. Event and interpretive word must be nearly one or the event itself may not only be misinterpreted, but even worse, lost, and therefore meaningless. Inspiration is therefore inseparable and indispensable as both event and word together are inscripturated revelation. Though there may have been prophets in Israel other than the ones who enter the pages of the Bible, and there most certainly were revelatory deeds in the life of Christ that are not preserved with an absolute interpretation for posterity (John 20:30; 21:25), normative revelation is Scriptural revelation. Without inscripturation, God's call of Abraham, His providential direction and judgment of Israel, and most of all,

74

His incarnation among us would have neither definite record nor definitive interpretation (John 20:31).

This passing reference in regard to the incarnation, the culmination of God's revelatory events, demands further comment. There can be no question, in light of Hebrews 1:1, 2, that Jesus Christ is BOTH the supreme event AND final word of God's revelation of Himself: "God, after He spoke long ago to the fathers in the prophets in many portions and in many ways, in these last days has spoken to us in His Son. . . ." Jesus Christ is the final expression of revelation in regard to historic event as well as divine word as God Himself takes on flesh and enters into the flow of history. On numerous occasions, Jesus would indicate that the testimony of His deeds and words were one. They could not be divided and therefore we cannot choose between them any more than we can forget that the Bible, for the most part, is also event and word. In John 10:37, 38, for perhaps the most familiar statement in this regard, Jesus states that "if I do not do the works of my Father, do not believe Me; but if I do them, though you do not believe Me, believe the works, that you may know and understand that the Father is in Me, and I in the Father." In brief, nothing more can be uncovered of God as God has manifested Himself in Person, so to speak (John 1:1, 2, 14; 14:6). This is why nothing may or can be added to the last book of the New Testament--The Revelation (Apocalypse) of Jesus Christ. Jesus Christ is the epitome of the revelation of God's Person and Will as well as the culmination of God's provision of salvation through redemption. As such, He is the center of both history and revelation (see chapter 13) and thus subject to pre-interpretation (Old Testament) and post-interpretation (New Testament). This can most clearly be seen from Luke 24:27 in which we read of Jesus' teaching activity on the Emmaus road that "beginning with Moses and with all the prophets, He explained to them the things concerning Himself in all the Scriptures" [Old Testament] and John 20:31 in which John tells us that while Jesus had "many other signs" in "the presence of the disciples," "these have been written that you may believe that Jesus is the Christ, the Son of God; and that believing you may have life in His name." Thus the words and signs of the Old Testament are met and fulfilled in Christ. The word has preceded the event. In the case of the New Testament, Jesus had accomplished many revelatory miracles, wonders and signs, but not all of these are recorded and interpreted for posterity. Those particular revelatory events that are recorded and interpreted by John are done so by means of the Holy Spirit's guidance and inspiration that insures us of inerrant and inscripturated propositions that provide us real information and knowledge of God, His will for us, and His means of providing for our redemption in the historic crucifixion and resurrection of Jesus Christ.

This, then, is it! There is no additional revelation. Nothing more can be added to the revelation of Jesus, the Christ. The only Christ, however, is the Christ revealed to us in Scripture. This written witness of the life of Christ is the extension of His spoken word. One cannot accept the authority of Christ's life or message, or understand either, without understanding and accepting the authority of New Testament Scripture. The propositional revelation of the Bible is indispensable for a viable and personal relationship with the living and ascended Christ.

This brings us back full-circle to the question as to the nature of revelation: propositional or existential, definitively objective or subjectively personal? In actuality, this is a false dichotomy! Special revelation is both historic encounter of God with man and cognitive deposit of this as well as His will and redemptive purposes. Thus just as we cannot choose between Christ's deeds and words, nor between the Christ figure and the propositional New Testament, we cannot choose between revelation as propositional and God's self-manifestation! Special revelation is encounter via God's actual involvement or personal entrance into history, but it is also absolutely propositional or the historic encounter would be lost and normative revelation would be as ambiguous as the signs and miracles left unrecorded by John and the Holy Spirit. Thus in order for there to be a self-manifestation of God, which most certainly is what revelation is, there must be a cognitive deposit of His Person and Will that results in a personal relationship with Him. This is exactly what the propositional revelation of Scripture provides us.

This does not mean that we can say that something is true because the Bible says it (though in one sense we can), but rather that the Bible says it because it is antecedently true. The Bible is the means of knowing God and His will. It records God's self-manifestation and encounters with men because they occurred and are therefore true as far as their occurrence is concerned. In other words, reality takes precedence over the knowledge of reality. Knowing something does not make it to be so. Thus it is the historic crucifixion and the empty tomb that saves me, not the record of such in the Gospels and the theological explanation of such in the Epistles. Nevertheless, this does not eliminate the absolute indispensableness of the Gospels and the Epistles for my knowledge and understanding of Christ's work of salvation. But the objective events take absolute precedence. At the same time, the objective events become historically unknowable and therefore epistemologically meaningless if there is not absolute record and interpretation of the Cross in Romans 3 and Galatians 3 or of the Empty Tomb in 1 Corinthians 15. Thus, in Paul's words in regard to evangelism, "whoever will call upon the name of the Lord will be saved." But "how then shall they call upon Him in whom they have not believed? And how shall they believe in Him whom they have not heard?" (Romans 10:13, 14). The propositional Scriptures provide the possibility of hearing. They are the interpretation and inerrant record of God's special revelation that progressively culminates in His complete self-manifestation to humanity in the Person of Jesus Christ. The Scriptures, especially the New Testament, therefore, are the perpetuation within history of the apostolic experience and comprehension of God's pinnacle of revelation--the incarnate self-manifestation of Himself!

There are, then, no cold orthodoxy nor neo-orthodoxy alternatives. Revelation is both the historic and progressive self-manifestation of God in Jewish history, culminating in Immanuel, the Jewish Messiah, and the inspired verbal propositions of the Old and New Testaments. Special revelation, biblically balanced and understood, is both objectively cognitive and subjectively meaningful. Its truthful assertions do make a difference in life. Neither a practical bibliolatry nor a mystic, assertionless Christianity is viable. God continues to uncover Himself in the ongoing and living expression of Himself in the final, written revelation of the Bible. The events of historic revelation and the words of inspired Scripture together are special revelation. We turn, therefore, to the very important question as to the means and extent of the inspiration of Scripture, since special revelation as event and word is lost without it!

REFLECTION

1. Identify the relationship between general revelation and special revelation. Has general revelation ever been totally adequate for man's knowledge of God?

2. What is meant by "cold orthodoxy"? Can this really be a danger? Why is "neo-orthodoxy" not a viable option? Identify neo-orthodoxy's positive contribution to the subject of special revelation. Discuss.

3. Why must I "believe that" before I "believe in" God? In what way is revelation still revelation regardless of my "believing" in it? What two facets necessitated post-fall special revelation?

4. Define special revelation. Why must special revelation be both God's personal manifestation and verbal propositions?

5. What is meant when one speaks of a "mediated revelation"? Why is such necessary? Does this in any way warp God's revelation? Must revelation be exhaustive to be true?

6. Why is history so important for special revelation? Discuss this in terms of both Testaments. How is Jesus Christ the "final expression" of special revelation in terms of both event and word?

7. Why is the Bible special revelation? Why is the Bible absolutely indispensable? Why may not the Bible be worshipped? Why does the Bible itself not save us?

[1]Martin Buber, I and Thou, trans. Walter Kaufmann (New York: Charles Scribner's Sons, 1970), p. 55. Buber is Jewish and thus obviously not a neo-orthodox Christian. However, his emphases were very influential on Barth and other neo-orthodox theologians. See, for instance, Emil Brunner, Truth as Encounter, translators Amandus W. Loos, David Cairns, and T. H. L. Parker (Philadelphia: Westminster Press, 1964).

[2]This is not a denial of general revelation, the subject of the previous chapter. It is a denial of the feasibility of a natural theology based on philosophic arguments for the existence of God that is supposedly prerequisite for the acceptance of special revelation.

[3]John Calvin, Institutes of the Christian Religion, trans. Henry Beveridge (Grand Rapids: William B. Eerdmans Publishing Company, 1964), I, 13, 1.

CHAPTER VIII

INSPIRATION: BOTH HOLY SPIRIT AND HUMAN AUTHORS

> All Scripture is inspired by God
> and profitable for teaching, for
> reproof, for correction, for
> training in righteousness (2
> Timothy 3:16).

We have discussed revelation as event and word in the previous chapter. Our task now is to investigate "how" and "what is meant" when we speak of revelation as written word. It is one thing to comprehend the necessity of God interpreting His revelatory events, or predicting future events, but what does it really mean to say the "Bible is the inspired Word of God"? What exactly is inspiration? Does inspiration deal only with the content and not the final written statements in Scripture? If not, how are the words in the Bible both the explicit Word of God and the words of Moses, David, Isaiah, John, Paul, and so on?

Inspiration may be defined as the means by which God insures that the revelation of His Person, Will, and redemptive activity is conveyed by man in an originally inerrant communication that is restricted to particular documents. What does this mean? It means that the interpretation of God's past revelatory events (e.g. Moses' record of the God-initiated events in the life of Abraham hundreds of years before Moses wrote Genesis), and the written prophecy of future events (e.g. Daniel and Revelation) are originally written without error. This written or inscripturated record is then the very Word of God. However, this is a particular record and thus only those inspired, or God-breathed, writings are Scripture.[1] This means there are very few such writings. It means that this God-initiated written record is restricted to only a very few particular documents. These documents are the sixty-six books of the Old and New Testament—the Bible.[2]

"All revelation is 'incarnational,' immersed in human history and language."[3] Thus the problem we faced in attempting to decipher the nature of our incarnate Lord Jesus Christ as both divine and human in chapter four is a direct parallel with attempting to understand the relationship between the Holy Spirit and the human authors in the inspiration of Scripture. The

81

Scriptures certainly teach the confluence of the Holy Spirit and the human writers in the creation of God's written word. While God could have provided us a written record of His revelation and prophecy similar to the tablets of the Ten Commandments (Exodus 31:18; 32:16; 34:1), He chose the instrumentality of human participation even as He did Mary for the Virgin Birth of the Living Word, Jesus Christ. In fact, even the fifth commandment is attributed to Moses by Jesus in Mark 7:10. This is undoubtedly the most distinctive Scriptural illustration of confluence because God is seen as speaking each of the commandments in Exodus 20:1, not Moses, and because of the subsequent but unique reception of the Ten Commandments by Moses. Jesus also attributes the words of other Old Testament Scripture to the human authors themselves such as Isaiah (Mark 7:6; John 12:27, 38), and David (Mark 12:36), and Daniel (Matthew 24:14). It is clear in all these passages, however, that the authority of all these quotations is divine and not human.[4] The most distinctive perhaps of these references both authoritatively and in regard to the confluence of inspiration is the Mark 12:36 statement where Jesus says, "David himself says in the Holy Spirit." David's words, but nevertheless they were also the words of God by the Holy Spirit. One set of words, belonging to both God and man, though in different ways. God, via revelation, is the source of the insight that provokes these words selected by the Holy Spirit from the linguistic, cultural and historical parameters of the man, David. Thus David, as to form and not content, is in this sense the "source" of the words that God uses to adequately convey His Word through man to man and for man.

This interchanging of reference to humanly written Scripture as God's, or of God's direct speaking as simply Scripture, is common throughout the New Testament. The simplest statement of the human author is assigned to God as its true author and the direct words of God, recorded by the Scriptural writers, are referred to by the names of the human authors. For instance, in Matthew 19:4, 5 Jesus attributes directly to God the comment of Moses in Genesis 2:24 that a man leaves his parents to cleave unto his wife and "they shall become one flesh." The opposite phenomenon is seen when in Romans 9:17 Paul attributes to Scripture per se what is the direct speaking of God to the Pharoah of Egypt in Exodus 9:16. Paul does the same thing in Galatians 3:8 when he attributes to Scripture instead of God the blessing of the nations through Abraham's seed. For both Jesus and Paul there is no difference in quoting God directly or humanly written Scripture. They are equally authoritative for they are both the Word of God.

These references and illustrations certainly make clear the Bible's own understanding of the absolute confluence of God and man in producing the written Scriptures, the Holy Bible. The Bible is not partially God's and partially man's. It is a divine book. It is God's book! But it was physically written by men to people of their era and within the confines of the writers' and recipients' culture. This biblical balance in regard to inspiration was made quite clear by Benjamin B. Warfield in an article originally entitled "Inspiration" in The International Standard Bible Encyclopaedia, but now in his book The Inspiration and Authority of the Bible:

> That the Scriptures are throughout a Divine book, created by the Divine energy and speaking in their every part with Divine authority directly to the heart of the readers, is the fundamental fact concerning them which is witnessed by Christ and the sacred writers to whom we owe the New Testament. But the strength and constancy with which they bear witness to this primary fact do not prevent their recognizing by the side of it that the Scriptures have come into being by the agency of men. It would be inexact to say that they recognize a human element in Scripture: they do not parcel Scripture out, assigning portions of it, or elements in it, respectively to God and man. In their view the whole of Scripture in all its parts and in all its elements, down to the last minutiae, in form of expression as well as in substance of teaching, is from God; but the whole of it has been given by God through the instrumentality of men [italics added].5

The Scriptural passage that helps us the most to understand the "how" of biblical inspiration is 2 Peter 1:20, 21:

> But know this first of all, that no prophecy of Scripture is a matter of one's own interpretation, for no prophecy was ever made by an act of human will, but men moved by the Holy Spirit spoke from God.

This passage is not dealing with our interpretation of the Bible, as some have erroneously taught, but with the origin of Scripture. Verse 20 is simply affirming the fact that no part of Scripture is the invention or the product of human ingenuity. The Bible is not man's own interpretation of God's revelatory acts. Neither is it created simply by man's will as mere myth (2 Peter 1:16). It is God-initiated. Men wrote, but the content of their writing was of God's will and grace, not by the will even of divinely chosen prophets and apostles. The word moved (Greek pheromenoi) comes from a word that basically means to bear, carry, or come forth.[6] It is in a passive form connoting the Holy Spirit carrying or bearing the prophets along as they bring forth His word. Since both ruach in Hebrew and the Greek pneuma mean breath as well as Spirit, the idea of the breath of prophets being carried along by the Holy Spirit, the breath of God, is very expressive to denote the act of the inspiration, or God-breathing, of the Holy Scriptures. This is the only reference to the Holy Spirit in the epistle. But both the Holy Spirit and the prophets together produce the holy writings. Strachan, in fact, notes that "it is of much significance for the interpretation of the whole passage that anthropoi [men] occupies a position of emphasis at the end of the sentence, thus bringing into prominence the human agent."[7] The human author is thus prominent even in this passage that so clearly denies that man has anything to do with the origin or content of God's Word. This passage very distinctively proclaims the biblical balance we have seen above in Jesus and Paul referring to the written and authoritative Old Testament Scripture as "God said," "Moses said," "Isaiah said," and "David himself says in the Holy Spirit." This is the biblical balance that maintains that inspiration is both the Holy Spirit and human authors. Warfield concludes commenting on this passage in the same manner:

Here the whole initiative is assigned to God, and such complete control of the human agents that the product is truly God's work. The men who speak in this "prophecy of Scripture" speak not of themselves or out of themselves, but from "God": they speak only as they are "borne by the Holy Ghost." But it is they, after all, who speak. Scripture is the product of man, but only of man speaking from God and under such a control of the Holy Spirit as that in their speaking they are "borne" by Him[8] [italics added].

The above italics are obviously not done to deny or play down the absolute and indispensable role of the Holy Spirit in the production of the written Scriptures. However, the italics are there to emphasize the biblical balance of man's role in the production of the Scriptures. This role frequently needs to be emphasized for those of us who so firmly believe in the Bible as God's absolute, inerrant, and normative Word. We occasionally deny the humanity of the Bible in our practice and approach to it even as we unconsciously are embarrassed and even occasionally play down the humanity of our Lord. Just as there would be no salvation if Jesus was not fully man as well as fully God, so also there would be no Holy Scriptures, no propositional statement providing us true knowledge of God's Person and His Will for us, if there were no human authors for the expression of God's Word in human history.

The best biblical illustration of the relationship between the Holy Spirit and the writers of Scripture is the relationship between Aaron and Moses. In Exodus 4:15-16 we read these instructions from God:

"And you [Moses] are to speak to him and put the words in his [Aaron's] mouth; and I, even I, will be with your mouth and his mouth, and I will teach you what you are to do. Moreover, he shall speak for you to the people; and it shall come about that he shall be

85

> as a mouth for you, and you shall
> be as God to him" [italics added].

Aaron will speak. It will be Aaron's tongue that
enunciates the words. But nevertheless Moses will
really be the initiator and source of the words Aaron
speaks. Moses will speak in the language of Aaron.
Though they are brothers, Moses presumedly has a finer
education than Aaron. Perhaps he could speak in a very
refined Egyptian that Aaron could not master. His
vocabulary might be much broader than Aaron's. Unless
they were going to speak to Pharoah one phrase or
sentence at a time as in oral translation of a speaker
of one language to an audience of another language,
which cannot be ruled out though very doubtful, Moses
must have confined his message to the working vocabulary, etc. of Aaron. While this attempt at human
analogy is not perfect to encapsulate totally the
relationship of the human authors of Scripture with the
Holy Spirit, it is God that permits us to attempt to
use this analogy by stating that "he shall be as a
mouth for you, and you shall be as God to him." In
Exodus 7:1 Moses is told that God will "make you as God
to Pharoah, and your brother Aaron shall be your
prophet." Thus the relationship between Moses' word
and Aaron's word is similar, if not identical, to God's
Word and the prophet's in the inspiration of Scripture.
Jeremiah 1:9 sounds very similar to the relationship of
Moses and Aaron: "Then the Lord stretched out His hand
and touched my mouth, and the Lord said to me, 'Behold,
I have put My words in your mouth.'" Thus, like Aaron,
we hear Jeremiah's voice but receive God's Word as one
with Jeremiah's words just as the Pharoah received
Moses' word through Aaron. David claims the same thing
when he says "the Spirit of the Lord spoke by me, and
His word was on my tongue" (2 Samuel 23:2). This
identity of God's Word with the prophet's words is
divinely authenticated by the prophet's words being
fulfilled in regard to historical prediction (Deut.
18:18-22; note especially verse 19--"My words which he
shall speak in My name"). Jeremiah actually uses this
test of the prophet's words coming true to distinguish
between himself and Hananiah in Jeremiah 28:9: "The
prophet who prophesies of peace, when the word of the
prophet shall come to pass, then that prophet will be
known as one whom the LORD has truly sent." Jeremiah's, not Hananiah's, prophecy not only comes true in
regard to Judah's captivity by Babylon, but Jeremiah's
other prophecy did also: "This year you [Hananiah] are
going to die, because you have counseled rebellion

86

against the LORD. So Hananiah the prophet died in the same year in the seventh month" (Jeremiah 28:16b, 17).

The prophet's human words are thus identical with the words of God in the state of inspiration. But we may yet be unsatisfied as to the relationship between the prophet's words and God's Word since we still do not _really_ know how God's Word gets in the prophet's mouth. Neither of these issues are really speculated on in the Bible. There is one question that can be answered that will help us if not completely satisfy us. Can human words adequately communicate the revelation and words of God? Numerous theologians claim that finite words are incapable of revealing the transcendent and infinite God. Some go so far as to claim that we dishonor God by elevating something finite and human to infinite and divine status. But this is to argue in reverse. It is not that _we_ bring finite words to God, but that God comes to His prophets and apostles and provides them with true if not exhaustive knowledge of Himself by revealing Himself within their human limits. Theologians call this anthropomorphism. Calvin's famous statement is appropriate here: "God, in so speaking, lisps with us as nurses are wont to do with little children."9 Since God alone knows what He wants to communicate, He alone can choose the relevant analogies and proper words to communicate just those aspects of His Person and Will that He desires us to know. If He cannot do this, then He is not infinite. The Scriptures are not man's attempt to symbolize the spiritual realm as much of Protestant liberalism has taught for the past 150 years since Friedrich Schlierermacher's _The Christian Faith_. Rather the Holy Spirit sacramentally used facets of our frame of reference to adequately convey God's intentions for special revelation. Bernard Ramm puts this excellently in his book _Special Revelation and the Word of God_:

> God _adapts_ his revelation to this cosmos; he _mediates_ it at our level; he _gives_ it an anthropic character suitable to our language and mentality. It is therefore _assimilable_ by us, and what we can assimilate we can _assert_10 [original italics].

God's condescension to "lisp as a nurse with an infant" is by means of human words. All that we know

87

about God, the Trinity, Christ, the Holy Spirit, the Resurrection, Redemption, we know by means of the human words of the Bible. There is no Word of God separate from the words in black and white on the pages of Holy Scripture. These words must be trustworthy witnesses to themselves or they certainly cannot be the source of God's Word. The fact that God's Word is heard when these words on the page are read is what is meant by the doctrine of verbal plenary inspiration. That is, every word of Scripture is God-breathed. The very words are the words that God deemed appropriate to adequately and truthfully communicate to His fallen creatures. This does not mean that words are so exact they have one narrow meaning. Words function in an area of meaning. Nearly every word has multiple meanings numerically listed in a dictionary or lexicon. The relationship between words and meaning is dynamic. Meaning is flexible not mechanical. The same meaning can be expressed in different word order, synonyms (as every writer reaches for his thesaurus), indirect or direct discourse, etc. This is a truism for anyone who reads the Gospels. In a parallel manner, no one can read the Bible in two languages and not see this immediately! The same meaning is conveyed whether I read the New Testament in English, German, or Greek. This is why the New Testament writers frequently could quote the Old Testament from the Greek Septuagint rather than from the Hebrew and use it in the New Testament itself. It is not indifference to the original Hebrew, but the realization that God's truth is communicable in every language. This being the case, the debate in the English speaking world for the sacrosanctity of one particular version makes no sense whatsoever. There is no difference in meaning, only a subjective attachment, that I find when I personally use the American Standard Version in the college classroom, memorize the King James, and currently am reading through the Bible in the New International Version during devotions.

This does not mean, obviously, that there is no limit to the area of meaning of any particular word or that the relationship between meanings and words is not real. There is an absolute limit as to the flexibility of words, phrases, and sentences to convey the same thought. For words, limit is primarily fixed by context. Within their "context words are definable within such narrow limits that . . . they convey real ideas within acceptable limits of accuracy."[11] Since revelation can thus be expressed only within a restricted number of possibilities, the function or task of inspiration is to present and preserve revelation in a completely appropriate and trustworthy manner within these linguistic and verbal possibilities. R. Laird Harris continues:

> Precision and accuracy are not terms exactly equivalent to truth. The fact that a word cannot be exhaustively and precisely defined does not mean that it cannot be used appropriately to convey an idea, otherwise one should never be able to order a meal in a restaurant.

> To speak with some degree of approximation is yet to speak truly. The Bible speaks truly and conveys the ideas of God within normal limits of accuracy both to man and God. The admitted inaccuracy of words in approximation is no bar to communication upon earth nor to communication from God to man, nor is it a violation of the doctrine of verbal inspiration . . . . Just as men may know God truly though not comprehensively, so the words of the Bible reveal truth even though they do not speak with infinite precision.12

Thus, as John Frame concludes his articles, "human language _may_ convey the infallible word of God, because God is _lord_--even of human language!"13 [original italics].

This lack of "infinite precision" brings us to the facet of inspiration that is also the title of the book in which Frame's article is found--God's inerrant word. What is meant by "inerrancy"? In the above quotation Frame uses "infallible" as synonymous with "inerrancy" but others have attempted to separate these two ideas. The debate in evangelical circles over inerrancy has subsided a little during the last few years, but it is still very central to any discussion concerning the inspiration of Scripture.

At times this debate has become semantic as nearly the same definition and the identical illustrations (e.g. the mustard seed) are used by both those who claim the Bible has errors and those who proclaim the Bible inerrant. In regard to the mustard seed, for instance, the question is whether we must have literal and "infinite precision," or whether it is acceptable to speak in terms of approximation, normal limits of accuracy, and figuratively as Jesus no doubt did with regard to the poor little mustard seed (Matthew 13:31; Mark 4:31; Luke 13:19). Warfield, who was certainly one of the first to use the term inerrancy, simply meant the "entire truthfulness which is everywhere presupposed in and asserted for Scripture by the Biblical writers."14 Inerrancy then may be a relatively new word of the past 90 years or so, but the full trustworthiness of the Bible as to every facet on which it speaks and in regard to its complete inspiration is without doubt the historic doctrine of the church.15 What Kirsopp Lake, a liberal Protestant historian and theologian, wrote in 1926 is certainly correct:

> It is a mistake often made by educated persons who happen to have but little knowledge of historical theology, to suppose that fundamentalism is a new and strange form of thought. It is nothing of the kind; it is the partial and uneducated survival of a theology which was once universally held by all Christians. How many were there, for instance, in Christian churches in the eighteenth century who doubted the infallible inspiration of all Scripture? A few, perhaps, but very few. No, the fundamentalist may be wrong; I think that he is. But it is we who have departed from the tradition, not he; and I am sorry for the fate of anyone who tries to argue with a fundamentalist on the basis of authority. The Bible and the corpus theologicum of the Church are on the fundamentalist side.16

Biblical inerrancy, however, is not inductively provable. Given the 1600 years over which the Bible was written and the numerous incidents and facts it relates, this is an utter impossibility. Inerrancy is a statement of faith in light of the nature of God and the means of inspiration, not a scientifically demonstrable hypothesis. However, the exactness with which the Bible has been absolutely proven to be true by historical research and archaeological discoveries provides our statement of faith considerable empirical support.17 Neither does inerrancy eliminate the need of a reverent biblical criticism. Because the Bible is a human book it must be analyzed and studied as all other books within history.18 Inerrancy no more makes the Bible immune to historical and textual criticism by careful scholars than Christ's sinlessness denies His humanity and therefore His historicity. The problem of biblical criticism is not its necessary reality, but the way in which Scripture is treated by the human critic. While the Bible has its historical and human sides, it is not just another human work, but the Word of God in human form even as Christ was God in the form and likeness of men.

Inerrancy, then, is a consequent of the ultimate divine authorship and thus each particular of Scripture must be viewed in the light of the whole. The practice of maintaining apparent errors in the text as simple difficulties that will be clarified with additional information is not to play ostrich as liberals and even some evangelicals claim. Such an attitude and practice has been vindicated many times during the past 200 years. Difficulties do remain! Some are real, some are man-made by both sides because of a false criteria of scientific precision and/or extreme literalness.19 Nevertheless, the Scriptures are as "wholly true" as God's written incarnate Word as Jesus Christ is "wholly sinless" as God's living incarnate Word. This biblical balance of Scripture as both Holy Spirit and human authors is definitively expressed by Bernard Ramm:

> The Christian Church through the centuries has insisted that the total Scripture is at the same time the word of God and the word of man. Although written by men it is God's truth; and although God's truth it is the product of human authors. Their words yet God's word; and God's word is uniquely his word though in the garments of man's words.20

REFLECTION

1. Define inspiration. Relate inspiration to the questions of canonicity. Why is inspiration so integral to special revelation?

2. What is meant by the phrase "all revelation is incarnational"? How does Jesus illustrate this truth?

3. Explain the concept of confluence in regard to the historical production of the Bible. Is this a biblical doctrine itself? If so, interpret 2 Peter 1:20, 21 in this light.

4. Of what significance is the Moses/Aaron relationship to our understanding of the doctrine of inspiration? List and discuss other helpful illustrations of inspiration.

5. Identify the biblical test for distinguishing between false and true claims of prophetic inspiration. Illustrate the effectiveness of this test.

6. How may finite human language communicate God's Word? What is the role of the Holy Spirit in this enablement? Must a verbal plenary doctrine of inspiration result in an extreme literalness of interpretation? How precise must a word be to adequately convey true information?

7. Why is there so much misunderstanding and debate over the concept of Biblical inerrancy? Is inerrancy a new claim? Is it scientifically provable? Do such claims eliminate biblical criticism? Why is inerrancy so important to the doctrine of the scriptures?

ENDNOTES

[1]The Greek word in 2 Timothy 3:16 is theopneustos which is a compound of the two words for God and breath and thus literally means God-breathed. It definitely indicates that Scripture is a divine product, but there is no indication of how this is accomplished. This is why the doctrine of inspiration has been so debated for the past 100 years in Christendom, and the past 20 years or so even in evangelical denominations and schools.

[2]The identifying of these books in the past is called the process of canonicity. This term comes from the Greek word kanon, Hebrew kaneh, which literally means "measuring rod." Thus canonization meant that certain books met the "measuring rod" of being inspired of God. Canonization was obviously also a joint product of God's guidance and man's investigation, though it is not a subject of one of the chapters in this book. Speaking of the process of New Testament canonization, Lewis Sperry Chafer notes this duality by stating that "the way in which the New Testament canon was formed was wholly natural, and yet the thing achieved was as wholly supernatural." Systematic Theology (Dallas: Dallas Seminary Press, 1964), I, 92. We may define canonicity as the test by which men marked out those documents in which God has been pleased to provide us an inerrant statement and record of His Person, Will, and redemptive activity.

[3]Clark Pinnock, Biblical Revelation (Chicago: Moody Press, 1971), p. 29.

[4]The absolute authority of the Old Testament Scriptures, implying that God is the author, is never questioned by Jesus. On numerous occasions Christ simply refers to the "Scripture" or "Scriptures" as absolute (Matthew 21:42; 26:54; John 5:39; 7:38). This absolute written authority of Scripture is also seen by phrases such as "have you not read" (Matthew 12:5; 9:4; 21:16; 22:31) and "it is written" (Matthew 11:10; 21:13; 26:24, 31).

[5]Benjamin B. Warfield, The Inspiration and Authority of the Bible (Philadelphia: The Presbyterian and Reformed Publishing Company, 1948), p. 150.

[6]George Liddell and Robert Scott, A Greek-English Lexicon, ninth edition (Oxford: Clarendon Press, 1961), 1922-1924.

⁷R. H. Strachan, The Second Epistle General of Peter in The Expositor's Greek New Testament, edited by W. Robertson Nicoll (Grand Rapids: William B. Eerdmans Publishing Company, 1961), V, 132-133.

⁸Warfield, op. cit., p. 151.

⁹John Calvin, Institutes of the Christian Religion, trans. Henry Beveridge (Grand Rapids: William B. Eerdmans Publishing Company, 1964), I, 13, 1.

¹⁰Bernard Ramm, Special Revelation and the Word of God (Grand Rapids: William B. Eerdmans Publishing Company, 1961), p. 40.

¹¹R. Laird Harris, "The Problem of Communication," in The Bible—the Living Word of Revelation, edited by Merrill C. Tenney (Grand Rapids: Zondervan Publishing House, 1968), p. 90.

¹²Ibid., p. 91.

¹³John M. Frame, "God and Biblical Language: Transcendence and Immanence," God's Inerrant Word, edited by John Warwick Montgomery (Minneapolis: Bethany Fellowship, 1974), p. 175.

¹⁴Warfield, op. cit., p. 173.

¹⁵This introductory book cannot trace the history of the doctrines of inspiration and inerrancy. Nearly all books dealing with the doctrine of the Scriptures will include such a chapter. One might see two books already noted in these footnotes: Benjamin B. Warfield, The Inspiration and Authority of the Bible, pp. 105-128 and Clark Pinnock, Biblical Revelation, pp. 147-174. For two excellent anthologies either defending inerrancy or refuting errancy, both edited by Norman L. Geisler, see Inerrancy (Grand Rapids: Zondervan Publishing House, 1979) and Biblical Errancy: An Analysis of Its Philosophical Roots (Grand Rapids: Zondervan Publishing House, 1981).

¹⁶Kirsopp Lake, The Religion of Yesterday and Tomorrow (Boston: Houghton Mifflin, 1926), p. 61.

¹⁷Archaeological evidence cannot be presented here. There are numerous fine books that provide this evidence. It is interesting to note that non-believing archaeologists admit that the Bible has a very unusual

degree of historical and descriptive exactness.   See, for instance, William Foxwell Albright, From the Stone Age to Christianity, second edition (New York: Doubleday Anchor Books, 1957).

[18]Like archaeology, this book can only point elsewhere for guidance as to reverent biblical criticism.   One such book I have found helpful in an introductory fashion is George Eldon Ladd, The New Testament and Criticism (Grand Rapids: William B. Eerdmans Publishing Company, 1967).

[19]J. I. Packer, "Fundamentalism" and the Word of God (Grand Rapids: William B. Eerdmans Publishing Company, 1972), pp. 94-101.

[20]Ramm, op. cit., p. 179.

CHAPTER IX

TESTAMENTS: BOTH CONTINUITY

AND DISCONTINUITY

The last two chapters dealing with special
revelation and the inspiration of Scripture that
identifies God's revelation with the Holy Scriptures,
His living and spoken Word with the written and
historical word of prophet and apostle, is the under-
pinning and lodestar of sound doctrine. Deviation here
will almost always bring about a deterioration of
apostolic doctrine elsewhere, be it a denial of Jesus'
deity, the loss of a redemptive atonement, or the
giving-up of the "blessed hope" of our Lord's literal
return. Among those Christians which absolutely affirm
each of these doctrines, there is yet a very troublesome issue, yea even a divisive one, that creates both
theological controversy and denominational differences
among evangelicals and fundamentalists. This is the
issue as to the relationship between the Old and New
Testaments of the Bible.

For the most part this is a problem of hermeneutics. Hermeneutics is "the science that teaches us the
principles, laws, and methods of interpretation[1]
[original italics]. How do we interpret the Bible? Is
the Bible to be interpreted like any other book? Do we
understand the Bible literally or allegorically by
seeking a hidden or deeper meaning of Scripture? What
role does culture, grammar, and history individually
play in comprehending the message of the Bible? These
rather technical questions cannot be dealt with here,
but one's understanding of the relationship between the
testaments will be affected by the answers given to
these questions.[2] It doubtless is obvious to the
reader by this point that the Bible has been interpreted throughout the previous chapters literally,
within the context and confines of its cultural and
historical milieu, with particular attention paid to
the meaning of words and grammatical construction.
This must be the case. The Bible is God's Word, but it
has been placed on man's tongue and therefore is no
different from other books in regard to cultural
coloring, historical context, and expression in the
given linguistic structure of Aramaic, Hebrew, or
Greek.

But even where there are basic agreements on the means and principles of interpretation, there is not evangelical unanimity as to the relationship between the testaments. No biblicist sees a division as radical as Marcion in the second century that posited two gods: one the tyrannical and arbitrary God of the Old Testament; the other the loving and gracious One seen in the Lord Jesus. While this may still be espoused by a very few of the most liberal preachers in Christendom, it is neither biblical nor Christian. However, theological orientation and denominational traditions make it very hard sometimes for those who agree on the great truths of the Bible, and without doubt maintain allegiance to the same Lord, to agree on the relationship between Old Testament Israel and the New Testament Church, to understand the great covenants of the Old Testament as completely fulfilled or yet awaiting at least partial fulfillment, and perhaps most importantly, to properly relate and differentiate Law and Grace.

There are two primary schools of theological interpretation in the conservative Christian world. These are usually labeled covenant and dispensational theology. The latter, for the most part, is predominant in those denominations and fellowships that were created by the fundamentalist controversies during the 1920s. The former is most generally found in those Reformed denominations that for one reason or another did not suffer doctrinal deviations in the first quarter of the twentieth century.[3] Dispensationalists have at times seen so much discontinuity between the biblical testaments that Law and Grace are totally antithetical to one another and thus even portions of the New Testament are thought to be inapplicable for the present era of grace. On the other hand, covenantal theologians often see continuity to such an extent that they identify Israel and the Church of Jesus Christ, thus functionally dismissing any literal and normal reading of large portions of the Old Testament and threatening themselves with the Galatian heresy. Dispensationalists tend to make all kingdom references in the Gospels yet future, covenantists usually, if not always, refer the kingdom promises to the present. While there is definitely a both/and mediating point to this _particular_ issue as we shall see in chapter thirteen, is there a similar mediating position to the continuity/discontinuity issue of the testaments between these two theological orientations? I believe there is! This position may not be as internally consistent as either of the other two positions, but it does attempt to maintain the biblical doctrine of fulfillment in Christ and thus continuity between the Old and New Testaments. At the same time, this both/and position does not forget that the Old Testament is also preparatory and progressive and that the incarnation of God's Son is not only the completion of the promises to the fathers, but is something new and final and thus there is also a real discontinuity between the testaments.

There are numerous facets to this continuity and discontinuity debate. Like most debates (be they economic or political, philosophic or theological), there is a modicum of truth but a partial perspective in both houses. This chapter cannot in any manner be exhaustive in regard to examining the many nuances of the question. We can, however, succinctly examine what most would consider three of the primary concerns in this debate: the meaning and scope of the Abrahamic and New Covenants, the relationship of the Mosaic Law to the Christian believer and Grace to the Old Testament saint, and the continuity and/or testamental discontinuity of the work of the Holy Spirit in regard to individual salvation.

The statement of the Abrahamic covenant is found primarily in Genesis 17:1-21, and to some extent in Genesis 12:1-3 as well as 15:4-21 where the actual "cutting" of the covenant is recorded. Our interest is primarily in the unconditional and eternal characteristics of this covenant, therefore verses 7 and 19 in chapter 17:

> "And I will establish My covenant between Me and you and your descendants after you throughout their generations for an everlasting covenant, to be God to you and to your descendants after you. . . . Sarah your wife shall bear you a son, and you shall call his name Isaac; and I will establish My covenant with him for an everlasting covenant for his descendants after him."

A literal reading of this covenant would not only establish its eternal duration, but also its unconditional nature. That is, this promise to Abraham,

Isaac, and their descendants is not contingent upon their faithfulness and obedience to the covenant-Provider. The arrangement providing God's continued blessing and watchful care is dependent solely on God's initial grace and sovereign will, not on the inherent merit nor the collective lifestyle of the Jewish people. Without doubt, some of God's promises to Israel were contingent upon their personal devotion and compliance to the divine will. The Mosaic Covenant is surely a case in point (Leviticus 26:1-45). But Psalm 105:7-11 states both that God "has remembered his covenant forever" and confirmed it "as an everlasting covenant." Walter C. Kaiser, noted Old Testament scholar, therefore states in his recent book <u>Toward an Old Testament Theology</u>, "for Abraham obedience was not a condition of the covenant."[4]

This being the case, it means that the physical nation of Israel, the Jews, are <u>still</u> the subject of God's care and special interest. The Abrahamic Covenant and therefore the Jewish people have two primary purposes: first, to provide and be a people of praise (Genesis 49:8; Romans 2:17-20; 9:3-5), and secondly, to be the necessary means of bringing God's Son, our salvation, into history (Matthew 1:1-17). While Jesus, the Christ, must have physical parents and therefore a human lineage if He is to be truly man and really the Second Adam (this being what the Old Testament both promises and traces), God's promises to Abraham are not exhausted with the triumphant ascension of our Lord to heaven. On the basis of His absolute covenant to Abraham God does not set aside Abraham's children even though they have rejected their heritage, Immanuel (Romans 11:1-5, 25-29), because <u>this</u> <u>is</u> <u>not</u> <u>their</u> <u>only</u> <u>reason</u> <u>for</u> <u>existence</u>. Thus the many idyllic passages of the Old Testament that picture peace and contentment <u>for</u> <u>Israel</u> cannot be so easily brushed aside and made simply to refer to the present era, or Christ's rule in the believer's heart, by any grammatical-historical exposition of the Bible that claims to be a literal interpretation of Holy Scripture. This does not mean figures of speech and obvious symbolism is crassly ignored or obviously destroyed. It does mean passages such as Isaiah 11:1-10; 54:1-55:5; 65:17-25; Ezekiel 34:11-31; 36:8-28; 37:1-28, to enumerate only a few, are either yet future, for Israel, and probably to be identified with Revelation 20:1-6, or any consistent and literal hermeneutic is seemingly dismissed.

But the biggest disagreement between covenant and dispensational theologians usually centers around yet another Old Testament covenant, the New Covenant, recorded in Jeremiah 31:31-34 and at least partially interpreted in Hebrews 8:7-12. The Jeremiah account proclaims:

> "Behold, days are coming," declares the Lord, "when I will make a new covenant with the house of Israel and with the house of Judah, not like the covenant which I made with their fathers in the day I took them by the hand to bring them out of the land of Egypt, My covenant which they broke, although I was a husband to them," declares the Lord. "But this is the covenant which I will make with the house of Israel after those days," declares the Lord, "I will put My law within them, and on their heart I will write it; and I will be their God, and they shall be My people. And they shall not teach again, each man his neighbor and each man his brother, saying 'Know the Lord,' for they shall all know Me, from the least of them to the greatest of them," declares the Lord, "for I will forgive their iniquity, and their sin I will remember no more."

At the Last Supper Jesus makes reference to this covenant with Israel and Judah when he remarks, before taking the cup, "this cup which is poured out for you is the new covenant in My blood" (Luke 22:20; see also 1 Corinthians 11:25).[5] Hebrews 8:7-12 leaves little doubt that while this passage is to be understood to be partially fulfilled in the present "Christian era," there awaits a still greater fulfillment. It is the same at the Last Supper. He speaks of never again sharing the fruit of the vine with His disciples until the "kingdom of God comes" (Luke 22:18; see also Matthew 26:29; Mark 14:25). This may not necessarily have to be the millennium, but it surely is to be understood as both futuristic and literal. And, in light of the New Covenant that is for both the "house of Israel and the house of Judah" (Jeremiah 31:31), and the hope of the excited disciples on the mountain prior to the Ascension where they received neither reprimand nor corrected instruction but encouragement in regard to their question concerning the kingdom's coming reality on behalf of Israel (Acts 1:6, 7), there is increasing credibility to the total fulfillment of those idyllic passages of the prophets of Israel.

It should be noted that Jeremiah does not say "I am now making a new covenant," but the "days are coming when I will make a new covenant with the house of Israel and with the house of Judah" [italics added]. Jesus identifies this with "the new covenant in My blood" (Luke 22:20). This certainly demonstrates continuity between the testaments. These are the "last days" from the perspective of the Old Testament as they are post-Messiah, even as Peter affirms at Pentecost (Acts 2:15-18, 33). The New Covenant is not forgotten, and therefore discontinuity, but it is initiated and therefore continuity is definitely established. Likewise, Hebrews 8 holds out a future aspect to this covenant at which time "all shall know Me, from the least to the greatest of them" (Hebrews 8:11). This too is demonstrative of continuity by holding out a literal and historical dimension to God's Kingdom on behalf of Israel identical with the Hebrew prophets. It may be chronologically discontinuous after 2,500 plus years, but it is in substantive continuity with the hope of ancient Israel. The present era when Gentiles are grafted into God's olive tree (Romans 11:17-24), and Christ has reconciled both Jew and Gentile "in one body to God through the cross" (Ephesians 2:16), may appear, and actually be, discontinuous. But this is not the end. Paul also knows of a greater theological continuity when he refers to the New Covenant itself in Romans 11:25-27. He writes: "a partial hardening has happened to Israel until the fulness of the Gentiles has come in," but eventually "all Israel will be saved" because "the Deliverer will come from Zion, He will remove ungodliness from Jacob, and this is My covenant with them, when I take away their sins." This is the essence of theological continuity between the Old and New Testaments of our Bible.6

More could be written here, and is written in chapter thirteen concerning the two-fold nature of the New Covenant. Therefore, we turn to even a more troublesome problem of testamental relationship--Law and Grace. The problem here is dichotomous and rather complex. Some have such continuity between the Old and New Testaments, especially in regard to Law, that one could question whether anything truly new occurred with the coming of Christ. Others so separate Grace from the Old Testament that Law and Grace are made to be antithetical in the extreme and thus there is almost total discontinuity between the testaments. Contrary to popular opinion, though both of the above practices are overstatements and therefore in error, the greater danger is the elimination of grace from the Old Testament.

This latter problem stems, at least in American Christianity, from a very influential pamphlet near the turn of the century, C. I. Scofield's Rightly Dividing the Word of Truth.[7] The premise is correctly set on 2 Timothy 2:15, though perhaps over-emphasizing the KJV translation of "rightly dividing the word of truth" [italics added]. The NASV translates this phrase "handling accurately the word of truth," the NIV by "who correctly handles the word of truth."[8] Scofield rightly wrote that "law, in the sense of some revelation of God's will, and grace, in the sense of some revelation of God's goodness, have always existed, and to this Scripture abundantly testifies"[9] [original italics]. It is also correct to characterize the period from Sinai to Calvary by "the law," even "as grace dominated, or gives its peculiar character to, the dispensation which begins at Calvary."[10] It is equally correct to say that Scripture never "mingles these two principles"[11] [original italics]. That is, one is not saved and made right with God at any time by either ritualistic obedience or legalistic lifestyle. God does "not delight in sacrifice," but "a broken and a contrite heart, O God, Thou wilt not despise" (Psalm 51:16, 17; see also 1 Samuel 15:22 and Psalm 40:6). However, if grace is theoretically always a facet of God's revelation, it may be overlooked and functionally dismissed when studying the Old Testament, if not by Scofield himself, by many of his twentieth century followers, when we read:

> Law always has a place and work distinct and wholly diverse from that of grace. Law is God prohibiting and requiring. Grace is God beseeching and bestowing. Law is a ministry of condemnation; grace of forgiveness. Law curses,

> grace redeems from that curse. Law
> kills; grace makes alive. Law
> shuts every mouth before God; grace
> opens every mouth to praise him.
> Law puts a great and guilty
> distance between man and God; grace
> makes guilty man nigh to God. . . .
> Law says, Do and live; grace,
> Believe and live. . . . Law is a
> system of probation; grace of
> favor. Law stones an adulteress;
> grace says, 'Neither do I condemn
> thee: go and sin no more.'[12]

It is of course true that the <u>work</u> of law is
"wholly diverse from grace." But many have read this
to mean that law and grace have absolutely no relationship with one another and thus the New Testament alone,
for all practical purposes, is the Christian Scrip-
tures. <u>This</u> is <u>total</u> <u>discontinuity</u>. Very few sermons
are heard from the Old Testament. It is as if the New
Testament not only completed, but made irrelevant, the
Old Testament. It is not simply a question as to the
discontinuity of the Mosaic Law because we "were made
to die to the Law through the body of Christ, that you
might be joined to another, to Him who was raised from
the dead, that we might bear fruit for God" (Romans
7:4). Under the heading, "Delivered from the Law,"
Lewis Sperry Chafer seems to nearly imply two God-
ordained means for salvation and thus absolute discontinuity. He writes:

> the law stands as the represen-
> tation of the merit system—that
> arrangement which, according to the
> New Testament, is held as the
> antipodes of God's plan of salva-
> tion by grace. Beyond the truth
> that both systems are ordained of
> God for application in such ages as
> He may elect, they set up contrasts
> at every point. The fact that,
> under the new order, the Law
> principle is done away as having
> nothing to contribute to the
> outworking of the principle of
> grace (cf. Rom. 11:6; 4:4-5; Gal.
> 5:4), should not create the
> impression that the law did not
> originate with God; that it is not

holy, just, and good; or that it
had not had His sanction.13

There is certainly no quarreling with the contention that law and grace are "antipodes," or complete
contraries, and thus diametrically opposed. The
quarrel is with the idea that the corruption of the law
and sacrifices into a merit and ritualistic system was
the "God-ordained system" for any age rather than the
perversion of God's gracious provision for man's
desperate plight. The Law was not given so that man
might "earn" salvation by merit through legalistic
obedience and cultic practices. The law was given to
reveal and demonstrate the sinfulness of sin (Romans
5:13, 14). The sacrifices were given so that man might
vividly recognize both the penalty of sin and the means
of its covering--death! (See Romans 5:12 and Ezekiel
18:20 as well as Matthew 26:28; Romans 3:24, 25;
Hebrews 9:22.) Jews were not part of the believing
remnant if they simply "kept the law" externally, going
daily to the temple, observing every sacrifice, but
with no personal commitment or devotion. The Pharisees
of Christ's time were directly attacked by Christ for
reducing Jewish worship to a merit system. Similarly,
Judah, prior to captivity, had for the most part
maintained the religious and cultural trappings of
Jewishness. Quoting Isaiah 29:13, first written to
Judah, Jesus labels these Pharisees "hypocrites," for
"this people honors Me with their lips, but their heart
is far from Me" (Matthew 15:8). Paul attacks this also
in Romans 2:28-29 when he writes that "he is not a Jew
who is one outwardly; neither is circumcision that
which is outward in flesh. But he is a Jew who is one
inwardly; and circumcision is that which is of the
heart, by the Spirit, not by the letter; and his praise
is not from men, but from God."

Thus the greatest danger in the discontinuity of
law and grace is not the absence of law in the New
Testament, but the denial of saving grace in the Old
Testament. While it is true, as Scofield contended,
that "law is God prohibiting and requiring," a "ministry of condemnation," are these only Old Testament
facets of God's holiness? Are not men still prohibited
to murder, steal, lie, commit adultery, and covet? Are
we not still to be obedient to parents, having no idols
(1 John 5:21) and "no other gods before Me," including
money (Acts 8:20; 1 Timothy 6:10)? In regard to grace,
did not God beseech, bestow, and forgive in the Old
Testament? Were not Old Testament saints truly

redeemed and made alive (regenerated) because, like Abraham, "faith was reckoned as righteousness" (Romans 4:9)? Was not grace prevalent in the Old Testament, enabling David and others to open their mouths and "praise him"? If not, how can Christians explain the Psalms which are the peak of man's expression of praise and drawing "nigh to God" in grace? Both Paul and James remind us that the biblical assertion "believe and live" may be wrongly understood and misapplied by true believers (Romans 6:1, 2; James 2:14-19). James, because it "sounds as if" he is saying "do and live," has been frequently misunderstood, even as those who rightly say "believe and live" have been frequently misapplied. TO BELIEVE IS TO DO! As James reminds us, the demons in one sense "believe and live," but also "shudder," that is "tremble in terror" because they are incapable of righteous "do" (Living Bible). Thus "belief," if it has no such "do," is dead, being by itself (James 2:17).

This of course does not mean a merit salvation. This is not a works-righteousness. These who erroneously ascribe such to the Old Testament have a complete discontinuity with the New Testament. Jewish hypocrisy can never be made God's norm, however, but the realization that everything in the Old Testament presupposes God's Grace, which is actually the presupposition of the Law, does not mean there is no discontinuity in regard to the Law and its purpose between the testaments. Paul writes in Romans 10:4 that "Christ is the end of the law for righteousness to everyone who believes." The word for "end" (telos) means goal or purpose. Thus the Law has attained its purpose and goal, its end, when Christ comes. It is now the "last days." While Old Testament law and sacrifices were God's gracious provision, neither are to continue now that God has come in Person and redemption and propitiation are provided in actuality not in shadow (Romans 3:24, 25). The law has been "tutor to lead us to Christ," but now that the actuality has come, "we are no longer under a tutor" (Galatians 3:24, 25). Even as "now we see in a mirror dimly, but then face to face" (1 Corinthians 13:12), so the law has finished its task and we are free of its guidance since the nature and total revelation of God is now manifest. This does not, however, mean lawlessness, or what is called in church history, antinomianism. The law is still of absolute moral significance. Except now, for the believer in Christ, it is not the Ten Commandments per se, or as such, but the "law of Christ" (1 Corinthians

9:20, 21; Galatians 6:2). In the 1 Corinthians passage, Paul definitely claims that he is not "under the Law," and that while he may for evangelistic purposes function as if he is "without law," he is never "without the law of God" for he is "under the law of Christ." The New Testament believer, like the Old Testament believer, is never "declared righteous" by law. Nevertheless, he is still in need of moral guidance. But his moral guidance is not Moses' shadow law, the tutor, but the law of Christ. This law is the "law of love" (John 14:15; 2 John 5). But this does not eliminate the essence of the Ten Commandments. For as Christ answered the Pharisees, the entire Law and the Prophets depended on these two commandments:

> You shall love the Lord your God with all your heart, and with all your soul, and with all your mind.

> You shall love your neighbor as yourself (Matthew 22:37, 39).

This is the law of Christ! Jesus says it differently but really the same in John: "If you love Me, you will keep My commandments" (14:15; see also John 15:9-14). Or, "a new commandment I give to you, that you love one another, even as I have loved you, that you also love one another. By this all men will know that you are My disciples, if you have love for one another" (John 13:34, 35; see also 1 Corinthians 13:1-13). This is not a contentless love, a mere sentimentality. This "love is from God" because God Himself is this love (1 John 4:7, 8). This is the love (<u>agape</u>) that is God's gracious gift (<u>charismatos</u>) to His New Testament children and for which Jesus prays for us in John 17:26 while we are "in but not of" this world. Since we are commanded to love others because we love Him, both the theological and moral tables of the Ten Commandments are reinstituted as the law of Christ. The "law of love," then, does have moral guidelines. Morality does not change between the testaments. Neither does God's demand that we "shall be holy, for I am holy" (Leviticus 11:44; 19:2; 1 Peter 1:16). This is most obvious and succinct in Romans 13:8-10:

> Owe nothing to anyone except to love one another; for he who loves his neighbor has fulfilled the law. For this, "YOU SHALL NOT

107

COMMIT ADULTERY, YOU SHALL NOT
MURDER, YOU SHALL NOT STEAL, YOU
SHALL NOT COVET," and if there is
any other commandment, it is summed
up in this saying, "You shall love
your neighbor as yourself." Love
does no wrong to a neighbor; <u>love
therefore is the fulfillment of the
law</u> [italics added].14

The law of Christ is not legalistic but spiritual.
Therefore, at the same time Jesus announces the law of
love to His disciples, He also tells them:

And I will ask the Father, and He
will give you another Helper, that
He may be with you forever; that is
the Spirit of truth, whom the world
cannot receive, because it does not
behold Him or know Him, but you
know Him because He abides with
you, and will be in you (John
14:16, 17).

This enablement that Christ promises also raises our
third issue as to the degree of continuity and discontinuity between the testaments. That is, to what
extent is the Holy Spirit's ministry identical in the
new era and thus continuous with the Old Testament, and
to what degree is His ministry different and therefore
discontinuous between the testaments. Nearly no one
goes to either extreme here. Neither are the differences as theologically crucial. This can be seen by
the fact that the differences are frequently as large
<u>within</u> covenantal and dispensational camps as between
them. All seemingly have continuity to the extent that
regeneration is the work of the Holy Spirit in both
testaments. All likewise have a degree of discontinuity as the baptism of the Holy Spirit at Pentecost is
distinctly identified as what Joel predicted would
happen in the "last days" (Acts 2:17, 18, 33). The
question of continuity and/or discontinuity is whether
Old Testament saints are indwelled and sealed as New
Testament believers, or whether these activities and
ministries of the Holy Spirit are a part of the <u>newness</u>
of the incarnation and the fruition of the program of
salvation.

The verses quoted above from John 14 would seem to
indicate that if the disciples were then indwelt by the

Holy Spirit, they were ignorant of His presence and enablement. But even more telling, the promise of the Father's gift is future. "He will give you another Helper, that He may be with you forever" [italics added]. It does not sound as if the Holy Spirit in any way is indwelling the disciples at this juncture. But who would deny that they are regenerated? The disciples may have had misplaced expectations, but certainly they had saving faith. But it would not seem that they knew anything of the indwelling presence of the Holy Spirit. This being the case, there would be no way to claim that the Old Testament saints were indwelt by the Spirit except an argument that maintains that since they "remained in a regenerated condition, it must have been the Holy Spirit who kept them so."15 However, this is not only an argument from silence, but seemingly implies that regeneration is not a new birth and thus may "fizzle out." New birth is new birth whether the believers of the era prior to Christ were blessed universally with the Spirit's presence or not.

Another passage in John would seem to confirm that the Holy Spirit was not yet universally given to God's children. In John 7:38 John records Jesus as saying that "He who believes in Me, as the Scripture said, 'From his innermost being shall flow rivers of living water,'" to which John adds the following explanatory comment:

> But this He spoke of the Spirit,
> whom those who believed in Him were
> to receive; for the Spirit was not
> yet given because Jesus was not yet
> glorified (John 7:39).

Thus the giving of the Holy Spirit to the new era believers, Christians, was contingent on the glorification of Christ. John is without doubt implying more than the baptism or enablement of the Holy Spirit at Pentecost. Why would not such rivers of water flow from within if the Holy Spirit already indwelled true believers? Thus Old Testament believers must not have been indwelled by the Holy Spirit. It is either/or here. Either they were indwelt and such ministry from within was a present fact, or the ministry was lacking because there was no indwelling Spirit. The indwelling was yet future, a consequence of the finished work of the Messiah, Jesus of Nazareth. Frederick Godet, the excellent French Calvinist commentator of an earlier generation, to whom we have appealed before, writes:

Until the day of Pentecost, the Spirit had acted on men both in the Old Covenant and in the circle of the disciples; but He was not yet in them as a possession and personal life. This is the reason why John employs this very forcible expression: "The Spirit was not," that is, as already having in men a permanent abode[16] [original italics].

There is one final aspect that indicates why the indwelling of the Holy Spirit during the "new age," the "last days," is discontinuous with the experience of the people of God in the Old Testament. The giving of the Holy Spirit is the "downpayment," the earnest money, that the last days have really begun. This is the Messianic era! This is how Peter in Acts 2 interprets Joel's prophecy in regard to the Holy Spirit. Paul likewise affirms this not only in 2 Corinthians 1:22 and 5:5, but more fully in Ephesians 1:13, 14:

In Him, you also, after listening to the message of truth, the gospel of your salvation--having also believed, you were sealed in Him with the Holy Spirit of promise, who is given as a pledge of our inheritance, with a view to the redemption of God's own possession, to the praise of His glory.

The Spirit is the "pledge" or promise that the program of God will be totally completed, even as the sacrifices were proven to be significant and meaningful by their total completion in the death and resurrection of Christ. Thus believers are now "sealed for the day of redemption" (Ephesians 4:30).[17] God's Word will be eschatologically fulfilled for both the individual and the totality of the people of God. The Gift of the Holy Spirit is both the proof that the New Covenant has begun and the pledge that the New Covenant will be completed. In terms of the doctrine of last things, this means there is both an "already" and a "not yet." But we shall see more of this later. Here we can confirm the continuity of the Holy Spirit's work of regeneration in both testaments, if we must at the same

110

time admit that the radical newness of the Christ-Event also provokes a discontinuity because the long-awaited "last days" have begun.

At all three points then--New Covenant, Law and Grace, work of the Holy Spirit--there is continuity and discontinuity between the biblical testaments. This should be what we expected. Surely there is continuity if Christianity is actually a fulfilled Judaism. But at the same time, if Judaism is completed, or perhaps perfected, by the arrival of her Messiah, Immanuel, discontinuity is inevitable. There is no alternative. Neither covenant nor dispensation motifs, in their basic emphases of continuity/discontinuity respectively, are wrong. Each, in varying degrees, must see the basic truth, on at least this point, in the other position. There is no other way. Biblical truth in this regard, as in so many others, is two-sided. Since the Old Testament points forward to something new there must be discontinuity, but because the New Testament explicitly refers back to the past, there must be continuity. In other words, there are two testaments, continuous and discontinuous, but one Bible![18]

REFLECTION

1. Identify the similarities and differences of covenant and dispensational theology. Why is the relationship between the testaments so crucial to these respective positions?

2. Discuss the main provisions of the Abrahamic Covenant. Is this covenant conditioned on Jewish obedience? Why did God desire a people for His name? Is the Abrahamic Covenant fulfilled with the birth of the Messiah?

3. In what way is the New Covenant similar to the Abrahamic Covenant? Is the New Covenant completely fulfilled with the coming of the Holy Spirit and the beginning of the Church? If not, why not?

4. Did Scofield overemphasize the King James translation of 2 Timothy 2:15? Discuss the positive and negative contributions of Scofield's work. Pay particular attention to the quotation from Dr. Chafer. Is there a danger of eliminating God's grace from the Old Testament?

5. Is the Mosaic Law continuously relevant to the New Testament saint? Compare and contrast the law/liberty emphases of Paul and James.

6. Is it true to say that Christianity is a "love ethic"? What is meant biblically by this? Does this mean that the Christian ethic is subjective and normless as some contemporary ethicists claim? Pay particular attention to Romans 13:8-10 and James 2:8-12.

7. How does Christ's teaching make it improbable that the Old Testament saint was indwelled by the Holy Spirit? What biblical and theological understandings indicate that the Holy Spirit is a New Covenant gift? Why is it not surprising that the testaments are both continuous and discontinuous? Illustrate how this is true for each of the three primary issues covered in this chapter.

ENDNOTES

[1]L. Berkhof, _Principles of Biblical Interpretation_ (Grand Rapids: Baker Book House, 1950), p. 11.

[2]Additional books to the one above that are helpful in answering these questions are: Bernard Ramm, _Protestant Biblical Interpretation_ (Boston: W. A. Wilde Company, 1956) and Alan M. Stibbs, _Understanding God's Word_ (London: Inter-Varsity Fellowship, 1950). More recently, R. C. Sproul, _Knowing Scripture_ (Downers Grove, Illinois: Inter-Varsity Press, 1978).

[3]The major exception to these generalizations is the Orthodox Presbyterian Church that was created during the 1920s, but never deviated from a covenantal theology.

[4]Walter C. Kaiser, _Toward an Old Testament Theology_ (Grand Rapids: Zondervan Publishing House, 1978), p. 62. Kaiser does comment on the same page in light of Genesis 22:18 and 26:5, as well as Hebrews 11:8, that "faith had to be joined to works to demonstrate its effectiveness and authenticity."

[5]Only the Luke account would appear to have the word "new" (_kaine_) in the original text. The reference to "the covenant" would have presented no ambiguity to the first-century Jewish readers of Matthew and Mark. Because Luke is written primarily for a Gentile audience the adjective "new" is affixed for the same reason, the absence of ambiguity. This is no doubt also the case in 1 Corinthians 11:25 where the original readers were primarily Gentile.

[6]It could be argued, though I am not inclined to here, that the allegorical interpretation of the Israelite prophets as symbolic references to the Church is really the path of testamental discontinuity.

[7]C. I. Scofield, _Rightly Dividing the Word of Truth_ (New York: Loizeaux Brothers, first published 1896).

[8]The original American Standard Version of 1901 suggests in the margin the translation "holding a straight course in the word of truth." This surely implies a degree of continuity between the testaments in a much greater degree than some have read into the word "dividing."

[9]Scofield, op. cit., p. 34.

[10]Ibid.

[11]Ibid.

[12]Ibid., pp. 34-35.

[13]Lewis Sperry Chafer, Systematic Theology, eight volumes (Dallas: Dallas Seminary Press, 1964), III, 343.

[14]See also James 2:8-12 where the argument of the law of liberty and love is not an antinomian casting away of the moral law. It is interesting and important to note that the "apostle of faith and liberty" and the "apostle of works and legality" really hold identical positions on the continuity and discontinuity of law and grace.

[15]Leon J. Wood, The Holy Spirit in the Old Testament (Grand Rapids: Zondervan Publishing House, 1976), p. 70.

[16]Frederick Godet, Commentary on the Gospel of John, two volumes, translated by Timothy Dwight (Grand Rapids: Zondervan Publishing House, n.d.), II, 79.

[17]The sealing of the Holy Spirit is obviously the indwelling of the Holy Spirit and thus without indwelling the Old Testament saints were not sealed either. This does not imply the possibility of the loss of salvation, or doubt as to remaining regenerated, as we saw above. Since the sealing of the Holy Spirit is a sealing into Christ in light of Ephesians 1:13, we have further substantiation that the indwelling/sealing ministry is a new development of the Christian era. Therefore, our bodies replace the Temple as God's dwelling with His people is individualized during this era (1 Corinthians 3:16; 6:18, 19) rather than His communal dwelling of the Old Testament (Exodus 40:34-38; 1 Kings 8:6-11, 27-30; Ezekiel 11:23) as a step toward His bodily presence in the millennium (Ezekiel 37:24-28; Zechariah 14:1-4, 9-11, 16-18).

[18]An exhaustive book by this title, though very technical as it is the publication of a doctoral dissertation, is David L. Baker, Two Testaments: One Bible (Downers Grove, Illinois: Inter-Varsity Press, 1977). A more accessible treatment is provided by

Kenneth L. Barker in "False Dichotomies Between the Testaments," <u>Journal of the Evangelical Theological Society, XXV</u> (March, 1982), 3-16.

CHAPTER X

SALVATION: BOTH PROVISION AND RESPONSE

There can be no question that the central and primary purpose of the Bible is to provide knowledge of God's purposes and means of providing salvation, deliverance, to creation in general and humanity in particular. The fundamental dichotomy within Christendom between liberal and conservative Christians centers on the doctrine of salvation and the means of its provision. Was Jesus Christ, God's Son, made "sin on our behalf, that we might become the righteousness of God in Him" (2 Corinthians 5:21) or not? This doctrine of substitutionary atonement not only permeates the Old Testament in practice, but is the biblical picture of what "Christ our Passover" (1 Corinthians 5:7) has done for us. For some people during the controversies between modernism and fundamentalism during the 1920s, as well as for many "Christian" ministers since then, to talk of atonement makes Christianity a bloody religion which supposedly denies God's dignity and certainly is humanly incredible. It is really this latter facet of incredibility, tied to the denial of Christ's deity, virgin birth, and resurrection, that makes the biblical doctrine of salvation unbelievable for these individuals. When these three doctrines are denied, there can of course be no biblical doctrine of atonement and the possibilities of a real deliverance from the penalty, power, and presence of sin.

An answer to this apostasy is not the purpose here, though Peter instructs every believer "to make a defense to everyone who asks you to give an account for the hope that is in you, yet with gentleness and reverence" (1 Peter 3:15). Rather we need to discuss the scope of God's provision for us and its application to us as individuals. Here there is much debate, and occasional division, among those who absolutely affirm and accept Christ's substitutionary atonement. Questions such as "for whom did Christ die?," "are all men savable?," "is it really whosoever may come?," "am I of the elect?" abound and receive quite different answers, all of which claim a biblical basis. It would appear that at least some of our evangelical problems here are due to a lack of biblical balance between the sovereignty of God and the moral responsibility of creatures made in God's image.

This last sentence will be utterly rejected by many readers who have said "amen" up to this point. There can be no balance between God's sovereignty and man's moral responsibility, they will claim. Is not man as a grasshopper before God? And the greatest of human rulers reduced to nothing before Him? (Isaiah 40:22, 23). Rulers and ruled alike are, most certainly, absolutely dependent on the mercy and grace of God for our lives as well as our continued existence! The creature may never ask of the Creator "why have you made me?" But this must not mean, nor must it be so interpreted to mean, the denial of the very essence of man, the image-bearer of God, for in so-doing we detract from the very glory and honor of the One who is our Creator.

The fact that God holds mankind responsible for our evil deeds, <u>even when they are within the confines of His sovereign purposes and plans</u>, is absolutely clear in light of the fall of the first Adam and the crucifixion of the Second Adam. Unless we say that God made Adam so that Adam would sin and therefore God is ultimately the One responsible for the entrance of sin into the world, we must admit that God's sovereignty does not preclude human actions which are totally contrary to God's absolute or preferred will. Of necessity the essence of human personality, to be made in God's image, is creaturely and relative freedom. Adam <u>did not have to be disobedient</u> to God, but, obviously, in light of the results and consequences, he <u>did not have to obey God</u> either. He was the one creature free to obey or disobey God! Calvin says the same when he writes that Adam "might have stood if he chose, since it was only by his own will that he fell; but it was because his will was pliable in either direction, and he had not received constancy to persevere, that he so easily fell."[1]

Only the original pair had such freedom. The human will is no longer "pliable in either direction"! It is in rebellion against God and alienated and separated from His Word and Will. This separation, of course, illustrates man's relative freedom as God does not "force" or "make" His creatures to be obedient, though He obviously <u>could if He would</u>! But this is not a freedom which enables fallen individuals to voluntarily obey God. Man cannot obey God because he <u>will</u> not obey God. This is the reverse of God for man <u>would not even if he could</u> desire to serve and worship his Creator. This is not a bondage of our essential

118

created nature from the hands of an omnipotent and sovereign God, but a bondage of man's own devising that perverts his own original nature so "that he cannot move and act except in the direction of evil."2   Thus God fully recognizes and permits man's relative independence because of His very mandate to create a reality that exists in its own right.   God permits man's sin-oriented autonomy, but His creation-intention to have personal relationship with His personal creatures is not thwarted because of the God-initiated reconciliation in and through Jesus Christ (Romans 5:8-11).

The reality of man's responsibility for his deeds, which are of necessity a part of God's program for the ages, is also clearly seen in respect of the crucifixion of the Lord Jesus.   Peter proclaims in his Pentecost sermon:

> "Men of Israel, listen to these words: Jesus the Nazarene, a man attested to you by God with miracles and wonders and signs which God performed through Him in your midst, just as you yourselves know--this man, delivered up by the predetermined plan and foreknowledge of God, you nailed to a cross by the hands of godless men and put Him to death.   And God raised Him up again putting an end to the agony of death, since it was impossible for Him to be held in its power" (Acts 2:22-24).

There can be no denying that God's purpose and foreknowledge is the context in which wicked and godless (literally lawless) men put Christ to death by nailing Him to a cross.   The men do exactly what their evil hearts dictate, but they may do such only because it is within the confines of God's determined plan and omniscience of man's complete history.   But though God "knows in advance" the outcome of mankind's lawlessness, it in no way detracts from the free and responsible moral agency of the parties involved.   God's knowledge beforehand no more makes God the source or cause of mankind's Christ-rejecting, Christ-killing deed than God's prior knowledge of the end result of Adam's freedom of choice to obey or disobey makes God the author of human sin. Sin is man's choice, not

119

God's.[3] God's omniscient foreknowledge only makes such deeds historically certain not logically necessary. That is, the very definition of Adam is not fallen sinner, but moral, personal, and rational being. Nevertheless, the fact that Adam would misuse his freedom was a factual and historical certainty if not a deductive necessity by definition. Calvin recognized the difference between factual certainty and logical necessity when he writes the following: "that which God has determined, though it must come to pass, is not, however, precisely, or in its own nature, necessary."[4] In other words, it is certain to happen, but it is not absolutely necessary. That I get four apples when I add my friend's two apples to my two apples is mathematically necessary, but while it is quite certain the sun will be in the sky tomorrow it is neither logically nor mathematically necessary.

The reality of God's self-limitation because of His holy character and truthful word, as well as the full recognition of the external reality of His creatures, is clearly taught, as we briefly saw in chapter two, in Exodus 32:1-14. In this passage is recorded the episode of Israel worshipping the molten calf. God is pictured as desiring to destroy the entire nation and begin again with Moses (verse 10). But this is factually impossible for even the infinite God. God had sworn by Himself a covenant of promise to Abraham, Isaac, and Jacob. He could not break His factual and historical promise. He had made the oath because God desired "to show to the heirs of the promise the unchangeableness of His purpose" since "it is impossible for God to lie" [italics added] (Hebrews 6:17, 18). Neither can the promise that "the scepter shall not depart from Judah . . . until Shiloh comes" (Genesis 49:10) be fulfilled if God begins again with Moses of the tribe of Levi. Thus we read that "the Lord changes His mind about the harm which He said He would do to His people" (verse 14). This is probably the one episode of the redirection of God's will that presents real problems as there is no moral or spiritual change in the recipients of God's repentance. Nevertheless, it does illustrate God's self-imposed limitation. It may have been recorded for this very reason.

God's sovereignty is absolute, but it neither denies God's holy, loving, and absolutely truthful nature, nor does it run roughshod over God's personal creatures made in His image, the acme of the terrestrial creation. This does not mean that we limit God by our own existence and finite power. "No!" God limits Himself both from within because of the infinite perfection of His Being, and from without by the very fact He decreed to create in the first place. It is not a question of God not being able to do all that He can but, in light of this incident in Exodus 32, that He will not do all that He can. We might be able to speak of this humanly as "moral power over His physical power." Surely God could have physically destroyed Israel and have begun again with Moses. But this would have been a denial of Himself and His covenant commitment to Abraham, Isaac, and Jacob.

God's sovereignty is not detracted from at all by the sinful decision of an originally sinless Adam, or a fallen race of millions. But neither does God's sovereignty deny the creation of dependent creatures other than Himself but made in His image--moral, personal, rational. This means that man's deeds, be they good or evil, regardless of the omniscience of the infinite and sovereign God, are man's moral responsibility. This means that man's personality is not denied by making man a puppet that must either obey or sin. Adam's fall refutes the former, God's holiness and perfection the latter. This means that man's moral and rational capacities are not lost even in the state of total depravity, or if they are, we no longer have God's creation, nor can we have a propositional revelation that is ultimately significant, cognitively meaningful, and personally appropriate.

Man, then, can still comprehend, if not obey, God's revelation and law, and he still inherently searches for the dimension of his existence that is missing in his state of alienation from God and total depravity--a relationship with his personal Creator. Man, in other words, is still God's creature. Thus provision by God, like for Israel in the desert, both physically and spiritually, is granted. Not only does the rain fall on the just and the unjust (Matthew 5:45), but God has provided for the more desperate spiritual problem also. This provision must be universal or unlimited in scope, or the statement by Peter that God does not want or wish "for any to perish but for all to come to repentance" (2 Peter 3:9) is incomprehensible (see also 1 Timothy 2:4).

121

Much debate goes on between young theologians concerning the merits of limited atonement (believers only) and unlimited atonement (for everyone). There are difficulties with either view. Certainly a strong logical case can be made for limited atonement. If Christ paid the penalty for everyone, limited advocates argue, then everyone is freed from the penalty of sin. Numerous neo-orthodox theologians do appear to argue for this style of universalism, based partially at least, on Romans 5:18. However, limitists assert, because universalism is obviously untrue, Christ must have died only for the elect, or true believers. But Romans 5:18 need not be understood as if it teaches that every individual is actually justified because of the Second Adam just as each of us were condemned and made sinners because of the first Adam. Rather Romans 5:18 is a powerful argument for the fact that <u>all</u> <u>men</u> <u>can</u> <u>be</u> <u>justified</u> because of the universal and unlimited scope of the effects of Christ's death. As all were included in the fall of Adam, so all are included in the work of Christ. The nineteenth century French Calvinist, F. Godet, rightly states: "The apostle does not say that all <u>shall</u> <u>be</u> individually justified; but he declares that, in virtue of the one grand sentence which has been passed, all <u>may</u> be so, on condition of faith"[5] [italics added].

Aside from the negative argument that if Christ died for all, then all are saved, the weight of the biblical evidence most assuredly is on the side of God's unlimited provision for every one of His creatures made in His image. Very familiar verses like John 3:16 and 1 John 2:2 certainly imply that God's provision of a covering for sin encompasses the human race itself. Verses like Titus 2:11 which state categorically that "the grace of God has appeared, bringing salvation to all men" and Hebrews 2:9 "that by the grace of God He might taste death for everyone" leave no biblical foundation for a limited provision for man's sin. Paul instructs Timothy that because God "desires all men to be saved and to come to the knowledge of the truth," and because there is one God and "one mediator also between God and man, the man Christ Jesus," then Christ "gave Himself as a ransom for all" (1 Timothy 2:4-6). In light of the contextual argument of verses 4 and 5, there is no doubt that the "all" of verse 6 refers to the human race. Paul leaves Timothy no doubt of the matter in verse 10 of chapter 4 when he writes that God "is the Savior of all men, especially of believers." Thus while there is a difference in actuality, there is no difference in possibility.

This is the epitome of the unlimited atonement perspective. Not that all men are actually saved because Christ is the Savior of all men by His substitutionary atonement, but that all men are savable. All men have a provision for their sins. The provision is not necessarily an actuality. God made both moral and ritual provision for Israel by means of the Law and the sacrifices, but Israel frequently turned their backs on God's provision. There was no response of acceptance and/or obedience on Israel's behalf. The Law was there, but neglected or, even worse, forgotten. The temple, priests, and Levites were available, but Ahaz actually closed the temple and boarded it up (2 Chronicles 28:22-29:10). The provision of salvation is there. There are no unredeemable individuals because there is no redemption available. But, as Paul told Timothy, the provision alone is not sufficient, there must be a response. Jesus Christ is the Savior in actual fact of only those who "especially believe."

When we turn to the other side, then, of salvation, man's response rather than God's provision, we find another problem. How can man, alienated and at enmity toward God, ever respond? Mankind "holds down" the truth of God that can be seen external to them and known within themselves as God's creatures (Romans 1:18-20). In effect, man either turns his back on God and tries to forget Him as the prodigal son did his father (Luke 15:11-32), or shakes his head in God's face as he fights to be "his own man and do his own thing."

The problem is thought to be solved by the doctrine of election. God chooses some to be saved. This, however, seems to get us back to only a limited provision. That is, Christ really only died for those God chooses, not "everyone" of Hebrews 2:9 or the "all" of 1 Timothy 2:6. This, however, is to misunderstand the doctrine of election.

There are four primary views of divine election, certainly one of the most difficult biblical doctrines for our finite minds to comprehend. The first might be called double-election. That is God chooses both those He will save and those He will damn to eternal punishment. The very purpose of creation is to create and redeem the elect. The extreme advocates of this perspective speak of God's decree to elect individuals before He decreed to create the elect and non-elect. Thus a portion of humanity are created for the express purpose of damnation. Passages referring to Pharaoh's hardened heart (Exodus 7:13; 9:12; 10:1, 20, 27; 11:10; 14:8) and the birth of Jacob and Esau (Romans 8:13-24) are made to apply to individual salvation rather than the events of temporal history in the context of Scripture.

Election, however, is never explicitly contrasted with damnation in the New Testament. More importantly, such a view of God denies the creation of man in God's image in practice, if not in theory. Man becomes God's toy. God's sovereignty is emphasized to the total exclusion of the biblical motifs of man's moral responsibility and the universal proclamation of the Gospel which results in the denial of the Church's mission of evangelism. God's sovereignty swallows up the love and justice of the Personal God. Logic and system have taken precedence over Biblical exposition and theology.

More balanced in regard to God's sovereignty and man's moral responsibility is the view of election that realizes no one would be saved without God's intervention of choosing and enabling some to believe and be saved. Any idea of a double election to hell as well as heaven is totally excluded out of hand. Man is not God's toy. Rather God is gracious not only in making provision for both deliverance from sin and its just penalty, but also in making it possible for those who are separated and alienated from God to respond to His mercy and love. Since fallen humanity not only cannot do anything to merit God's attention and forgiveness, but will not even care to approach Him for such in their wicked autonomy, God changes the individual so that he may respond to God's initiative. Because the final end of God's purpose is the glory of God, it is to that end that He creates Adam and Eve, permits the Fall, and from among fallen humanity elects some to eternal life while leaving the rest to the just recompense of their sinful deeds. This is perceived to be neither unjust nor arbitrary, but simply a gracious and unmerited choice of the sovereign God.

This perspective may teach either limited or unlimited atonement, but more frequently the latter. A greater division within this view is the degree of response to the gospel that totally depraved individuals are thought capable of making. If total depravity is understood as destroying God's image in man, then the unbeliever not only cannot respond to the gospel in trust and obedience, he cannot even rationally understand its presentation. Regeneration is then understood to be prior to faith. In other words, an unbeliever is made a new creation in Christ and given faith before rationally understanding the gospel. This position attempts usually to build its case for regeneration coming prior to faith on Ephesians 2:8: "For by grace you have been saved through faith; and that not of yourselves, it is the gift of God." But the gift in view here is not faith but salvation itself. The New American Standard Version correctly notes this in the margin. The noted Greek authority, A. T. Robertson, points out that the demonstrative pronoun "that" is neuter in gender and cannot refer to faith but must refer to salvation.[6] Verses such as John 1:12 certainly indicate some dimension of personal response is necessary prior to regeneration and the "right to become children of God" (see also Ephesians 1:13).

A second orientation within this election perspective understands total depravity more relationally and less essentially and thus provides man the capability of at least intellectually or rationally responding to the gospel's call. In other words, man's essential being as made in God's image is not destroyed, but a relationship between God and the individual simply does not exist and cannot exist until there is a moral and volitional change in man. Nevertheless, man still has moral inclinations, is capable of personal love and relationships, and is rational and can comprehend a logical presentation of the gospel, even if he cannot comprehend it personally and spiritually (1 Corinthians 2:14). Thus the examples of intelligible preaching throughout the book of Acts are not in vain. Individuals may have no desire to turn from their wicked ways, but they do inherently know that such deeds are evil and therefore wrong. Personal relationships are not totally fulfilling until, like Augustine, sinners realize that "Thou hast formed us for Thyself, and our hearts are restless till they find rest in Thee."[7]

Thus while election is still the means that will permit wayward and autonomous individuals to repent and be converted, unbelieving humanity can comprehend the essential proclamation of the gospel prior to regeneration evidenced by their questioning of its truthfulness or by laughing at its supernatural implications similar to the philosophers at Athens (Acts 17:32) because of their secular and naturalistic assumptions. This election and total depravity perspective rescues the gospel from mysticism. It realizes that the gospel must be rationally comprehensible and evidentially true prior to regeneration or it cannot become such because of a spiritual change in the knowing subject. Faith is really both cognitive and personal. This is a very important distinction frequently overlooked by Bible expositors. The Greek word for faith, _pistis_, is translated by "belief," meaning something we must objectively and cognitively know, and as "faith" or "trust" as our personal or subjective response to the object of belief. Thus the theological term "faith" refers to both the objective events of special revelation which are the factual and historical evidence of God's redemptive activity in history and therefore the object of belief, and the subjective response of the person who reaches out in trust to the God behind the events and evidence. Biblical faith, then, is not exhausted by the intellectual facet of belief, but it is a prerequisite to the existential dimension of trust. Faith as belief only is insufficient, given the experience of the demons (James 2:19). One must not only comprehend the message but "throw one's entire being out upon the Lord." The latter is not possible without the work of the Holy Spirit in creating a new will and love by means of the new word provided in the gracious gift and work of Christ. Regeneration is not prior to belief as the other division of this second perspective on election would have it, but neither is faith totally the product of man as those who completely deny election would usually claim. On the basis of a rational comprehension, an intellectual belief prompted by the convicting work of the Holy Spirit (John 16:8-11), man desires to "turn" his life toward God but cannot (Psalm 85:4; Jeremiah 31:18; Lamentations 5:21). It is at this point that God brings about a new birth, a new creation with a new orientation toward holiness and trust and away from sin and selfishness.

The primary verse that seemingly defines faith in the New Testament, Hebrews 11:1, comprehends faith in this two-fold dimension:

> Now faith is the assurance of
> things hoped for, the conviction of
> things not seen.

The word for "assurance" is the Greek word hypostasis that we have met previously in chapter 4 in regard to the Person of Christ. When used personally it refers to the apprehension of reality by the individual. It denotes the personal firm and trustful confidence or foundation provided by the testimony of the Holy Spirit (Romans 8:16). The word for conviction, elegchos, translated in the King James as "evidence" and the NIV as "certain," pertains to the factual basis of evidence and conviction upon which the personal assurance is based. This is a believing that rather than simply a believing in (see chapter 7 on special revelation). Biblical faith is thus both objective belief and subjective trust, both the comprehension of the rational propositions of the Bible and the existential and personal trust in the One of Whom the Bible speaks. Man cannot do the latter without the former. But neither can he do the latter without the regenerating work of the Holy Spirit. This understanding of election and faith was apparently advocated by Augustine when he wrote in his work On The Predestination of the Saints that "no one believes anything unless he has before thought it worthy of belief."8 Thus we as unbelievers can intellectually understand the proclamation of the gospel, but we cannot plummet its spiritual depth nor accept it as true without the electing providence of God that provides the conviction and regeneration of the Holy Spirit. This perspective toward election does truly permit a human response to God's provision in Christ since man can at least comprehend the claims of the gospel. This is imperative in light of the biblical mandates of "whosoever will" and the necessity of hearing the gospel to be able to rationally believe, and to rationally believe in order to "call upon Him" (Romans 10:11-14).

A third view of election simply understands election as God's foresight of man's positive response to the gospel. This view is frequently on the verge of denying God's sovereignty in its attempt to maintain the doctrines of unlimited atonement, man's moral responsibility, and the freewill of man. It is at this latter point that this position actually goes astray. We do not have a free will in the sense that as unbelievers we can choose between God or self, Christ or sin. We are free--but only to be disobedient to

God. The capacity to choose God rather than self and sin was lost in Adam. This being the case, election cannot be God's foreknowledge of our choice of Him and then counting us as members of the elect community on the basis of our free choice. Free choice in this sense does not really exist!

This view has been adjusted and made more palatable for many by the concept that all men are free and capable of responding positively to the gospel because of the death of Christ. Did not Christ say "and I, if I be lifted up from the earth, will draw all men to Myself" (John 12:32). Henry C. Thiessen, the most noted advocate of this view writes:

> Though mankind is hopelessly dead in trespasses and sins and can do nothing to obtain salvation, God, by prevenient grace, has restored to all men sufficient ability to make a choice in the matter of submission to God. This grace operates on the will before one turns to God. God, in common grace . . . has restored to the sinner the ability to make a favorable response to God. Thus God, in his grace, has made it possible for all men to be saved. There is no merit in this transaction; it is all of God.[9]

The debate between this third orientation and the previous position relates basically to the meaning of the word foreknowledge (prognosis). The noun is found only in Acts 2:23 in relation to Christ's crucifixion as we have seen, and in 1 Peter 1:2 where it may not refer to the doctrine of election at all. There is no question of the relation of election and/or predestination with foreknowledge (as a verb) in Romans 8:29, 30, however:

> For whom He foreknew, He also predestined to become conformed to the image of His Son, that He might be the first-born among many brethren; and whom He predestined, these He also called; and whom He called, these He also justified;

128

and whom He justified, these He
also glorified.

The word for predestinate (<u>proorisen</u> from <u>protithemi</u>) literally means to "place before" or to "design before hand." Thus God has designed that believers are to be conformed to the absolute image of our Lord Jesus Christ. This goal is placed before us as the end product of our initial justification and our progressive sanctification until we are conformed as such, or in other words, glorified (see also Ephesians 1:11). We are thus destined as believers to receive our inheritance in Christ according to God's will and purpose of sanctification. Our limits are set. We will absolutely be conformed to the Lord of glory, our Savior, God's Son, the Second Adam.

There is still the question as to the meaning of foreknowledge. Scripture certainly indicates that election and/or predestination is based on foreknowledge. But the actual meaning of foreknowledge is greatly contested. Does it relate to prescience or foresight as the French Bible translates <u>prognosis</u> in Romans 8:29 and 1 Peter 1:2, or does it connote choice as God knows intimately those who are to be His. This latter meaning is obviously the understanding of the previous positions. From the basis of Greek word study, however, either understanding is possible. This is a case where theological assumptions and understandings in regard to the Person of God, the consequences of the Fall, the scope of the atonement, the role of grace, etc. will determine one's understanding of this doctrine. Whichever view of foreknowledge is accepted, we cannot undermine the gracious provision of God and the response of sinners who are still creatures made in God's image.

There is yet a fourth perspective, if a decidedly minority one, in regard to election. This might be denied to be a view of election by our previous advocates. But certainly both election and foreknowledge must be related to God's omniscience in which God knows the "beginning from the end" (Revelation 1:8; 21:6; 22:13). Since this is undeniably the case, then, unless we are to deny God's eternal omniscience, we cannot speak of foreknowledge as either foresight in an analogous way with ourselves, or as knowing and choosing in eternity past which is really one with eternity future for an omniscient and infinite mind. R. C. H. Lenski basically states this position when he

129

notes in his commentary on 1 Peter 1:2 that "the dating in 'foreknowing' or 'foreknowledge' is only with reference to us who are bound to time and not with reference to God who is superior to time. To subject God to limitation of time or to stop his foreknowing at any point of time is to make a serious mistake."[10] This doesn't deny knowledge of time-sequence, etc. to God, but it does absolutely rule out making God's knowledge, foreknowledge, choosing, and willing time-controlled and/or sequence bound as these activities and abilities most certainly are for us. The doctrine of election may be a case of making God in our image and then wondering why it is we have so many problems with this doctrine? This very likely is a case of not taking Calvin seriously enough, and if this perspective is correct, a mistake Calvin himself made, that "any description which we receive of him must be lowered to our capacity in order to be intelligible. And the mode of lowering is to represent him not as he really is, but as we conceive of him."[11] This is a dangerous statement if this is applied to our real and objective knowledge of God by means of His revealed attributes in Scripture, but it could be absolutely correct when Scripture attempts to reveal the activity of God in an anthropomorphic manner. The very context of Calvin's comment is the attempt to explain both God's anger and His change of procedures under the idea of repentance. Anthropomorphic expressions of God's actions in terms of human analogies always has infinite to finite difficulties. Election may very well be one of these.

The biblical doctrine of election is not left without meaning in this perspective. Rather it points to the actuality and certainty of a community of faith, a people of God. From before the foundation of the earth (Ephesians 1:4), this result was seen as already accomplished as the end is simultaneous with the beginning in the mind of One Who calls Himself the "Alpha and the Omega" (Revelation 22:13). To say that "God elects" is to speak of the beginning, to speak of "the elect" is to speak of the end. We get into trouble when we confine the mind of God to sequence and make His electing the cause of the election, the beginning as the source of the end. Election is thus not a causative force but a resultant way of speaking. It is not an explanation as to why and/or how individuals have been saved, but it is a statement by God, before the completion of history, of the absolute reality and facticity of an entire host of redeemed individuals. Like New Testament prophecy that tells us

130

of the certain completion of God's historical activity and redemptive program from this side of the eschaton, election is the New Testament way to tell us of the certain completion of God's historical activity and successful redemptive program from the other side of the eschaton. Election, in this view, is the Scriptural way of informing us of the absolute finality of God's program, not an explanation of God's methodology.

Whichever of the above election views one believes the Bible teaches, one must not deny that the Bible speaks of both God's initiative of grace in the provision of salvation and man's moral need and personal capacity to respond to God in faith. The Bible does not speak of salvation depending on the autonomous free choice of man, but neither does it teach that man is absolutely devoid of any responsibility in responding to God's provision of salvation. Fallen man is totally depraved. He does not and cannot merit God's favor. He does not consciously seek God. But man must be understood to be capable of response to God when God seeks man, even as Adam did in the garden. This may be only intellectual response which is the first step in biblical faith, or a volitional enablement that God provides for all man in Christ's finished work. But response there must be! This is the case or the proclamation of the gospel by apostle, evangelist, or preacher is not really proclamation. The question raised in response to the first great sermon of Christian history, Peter's at Pentecost--"brethren, what shall we do?"--is not only the question every evangelistic preacher desires to hear, but also demonstrates the biblical teaching that sinful men can in some manner respond to the gospel's call (Acts 2:37). This is the response of the sinner when he is "pierced to the heart" (or NASV margin "smitten in conscience") by the convicting work of the Holy Spirit "concerning sin, righteousness and judgment; concerning sin, because they do not believe in me; and concerning righteousness because, I go to the Father, and you no longer behold me; and concerning judgment, because the ruler of this world has been judged" (John 16:8-11).

REFLECTION

1. Why is freedom a prerequisite to moral responsibility? How do the fall of Adam and the crucifixion of Christ illustrate that men are held responsible for their sins by a sovereign God?

2. What is the relationship between God's foreknowledge and man's free and responsible moral agency? Why is the distinction between "that which is certain and that which is necessary" significant?

3. Discuss Exodus 32:1-14. How may this biblical illustration help us to understand God's omnipotence in relation to man's creaturely reality?

4. Must Romans 5:18 be understood in a universalist perspective? Why is it safe to claim "that the weight of the biblical evidence" indicates an unlimited perspective to the atonement? Discuss the question as to the scope of the atonement in light of the character and nature of God.

5. What must always be kept in mind concerning both God and man when considering the doctrine of election? Interpret Ephesians 2:8 and Hebrews 11:1 in regard to the question as to the order of salvation. What biblical evidence is there that men can rationally comprehend the gospel prior to salvation?

6. Why is there so much debate over the meaning of the Greek word <u>prognosis</u>? How does the understanding of the meaning of this word determine one's view of election? Is it possible, as Thiessen claims, that God has enabled fallen men "to make a favorable response to God"?

7. Is what is identified in the text as a "fourth perspective in regard to election" really a view of divine election, or a theological cop-out? Defend your answer. May we be in danger of "making God in our image" by our never-ending theological speculation concerning the doctrine of election?

ENDNOTES

[1]John Calvin, <u>Institutes of the Christian Reli-
gion</u>, trans. Henry Beveridge (Grand Rapids: William B.
Eerdmans Publishing Company, 1964), I, 15, 8.

[2]<u>Ibid.</u>, II, 3, 5. This in no way is an acceptance
of fatalism by Calvin in which "all crimes receive the
name of virtues, as being in accordance with divine
ordination," I, 17, 3.

[3]2 Chronicles 28:9-11 illustrates the concomitance
of God's sovereignty and human responsibility in a
unique manner. The prophet Obed says to Israel that
because "the God of your fathers was angry with Judah
He has delivered them into your hand," but <u>they</u> are
also personally responsible for slaughtering "them in a
rage which has even reached heaven" and for the very
contemplation of subjugating the men and women of
Jerusalem and Judah as slaves. The victory within
limits is God's, wanton killing and slavery are
possible but are nevertheless evil and the soldiers of
Israel are held morally responsible by God.

[4]Calvin, <u>op</u>. <u>cit</u>., I, 16, 9. The famous Protestant philosopher Gottfried Leibniz (1646-1716) makes
this same indispensable distinction "between that which
is certain and that which is necessary." "Every one
grants that future contingencies are assured since God
foresees them, but we do not say just because of that
they are necessary." Gottfried Wilhelm Leibniz,
<u>Discourse on Metaphysics</u> in <u>The Rationalists</u>, trans.
George Montgomery (Garden City, New York: Dolphin
Books, n.d.), XIII.

[5]F. Godet, <u>Commentary on the Epistle to the
Romans</u>, trans. A. Cusin (Grand Rapids: Zondervan
Publishing House, 1956), p. 225.

[6]A. T. Robertson, <u>Word Pictures in the New
Testament</u>, six volumes (Nashville: Broadman Press,
1931), IV, 525. See also S. D. F. Salmond, <u>The Epistle
of Paul to the Ephesians</u> in <u>The Expositor's Greek New
Testament</u>, edited by W. Robertson Nicoll, five volumes
(Grand Rapids: William B. Eerdmans Publishing Company,
1961), III, 289.

[7]Augustine, <u>Confessions</u>, trans. J. G. Pilkington
(New York: Liveright Publishing Corporation, 1943), I,
1, 1.

[8]Augustine, On The Predestination of the Saints in Basic Writings of St. Augustine, edited by Whitney Oates, two volumes (Grand Rapids: Baker Book House, 1980), V.

[9]Henry C. Thiessen, Lectures in Systematic Theology, revised by Vernon D. Doerksen (Grand Rapids: William B. Eerdmans Publishing Company, 1979), p. 259.

[10]R. C. H. Lenski, The Interpretation of the Epistles of St. Peter, St. John and St. Jude (Minneapolis: Augsburg Publishing House, 1961), p. 25.

[11]Calvin, op. cit., I, 17, 13.

CHAPTER XI

HOLY SPIRIT: BOTH HOLINESS AND ETERNAL SECURITY

Unlike the previous chapters dealing with the
Trinity and the Person of Jesus Christ, we are here not
concerned with the Person but the work of the Holy
Spirit. Of course, the work of the Holy Spirit is
vast. This work ranges from creation (Genesis 1:2;
Psalm 33:6), preservation of nature (Psalm 104:29, 30;
Isaiah 40:7), the inspiration of Scripture (2 Peter
1:20, 21), the conviction of sinners (John 16:8-11),
and the regeneration, indwelling, and sealing of
believers (John 3:3-6;   Titus 3:5; 1 Corinthians 3:16;
6:19, 20; Ephesians 1:13, 14; 4:30), as well as the
production of Christ-like Christians via His baptism,
infilling, and fruit-producing tasks (1 Corinthians
12:13; Ephesians 5:18-20; Galatians 5:22, 23). It is
these ministries of indwelling, sealing, and baptism of
the Holy Spirit that illuminate our eternal security.
But these same ministries of God's Spirit also assure
us that such individuals will be Spirit controlled,
fruit-producing, Christ-like and holy people. These
two, security and holiness, cannot be divorced. The
Spirit does not provide one without the other. These
are the beginning, means, and end of the believer's
life, the very process of sanctification. They are the
both/and of redemptive hope. They are therefore the
subject of this chapter that attempts to bring together
the two perspectives toward sanctification that divide
evangelical denominations. But first we must define
sanctification.[1]

The primary meaning of the word is "separation."
This "setting apart" is not only a separation <u>unto</u> God,
but a separation <u>from</u> the world. This is the meaning
of Jesus' prayer for His disciples, including believers
of every age: "Sanctify them in the truth; thy word is
truth."   In other words, God's Word separates us <u>unto</u>
truth and <u>from</u> the prince of this world, the father of
lies. Scripture, as truth, has a purifying function as
it brings one to God and concomitantly takes the world,
sin, and selfishness out of the believer. We see this
illustrated in regard to the cleansing and consecration
(sanctification) of the Temple during the reign of
Hezekiah. Before the temple could be "set apart" for
its proper role in worship, it had to be cleansed and
separated from the filth of accumulated neglect and
idolatrous practices. We read in 2 Chronicles 29:5,
15-19:

Then he [Hezekiah] said to them, "Listen to me, O Levites. Consecrate yourselves now, and consecrate the house of the Lord, the God of your fathers, and carry the uncleanness out from the holy place." . . . And they assembled their brothers, consecrated themselves, and went into cleanse the house of the Lord, according to the commandment of the king by the words of the Lord. So the priests went in to the inner part of the house of the Lord to cleanse it, and every unclean thing which they found in the temple of the Lord they brought out to the court of the house of the Lord. Then the Levites received it to carry out to the Kidron Valley. Now they began the consecration on the first day of the first month, and on the eighth day of the month they entered the porch of the Lord. Then they consecrated the house of the Lord in eight days, and finished on the sixteenth day of the first month. Then they went in to King Hezekiah and said, "We have cleansed the whole house of the Lord, the altar of burnt offering with all of its utensils, and the table of showbread with all of its utensils. Moreover, all the utensils which King Ahaz had discarded during his reign in unfaithfulness, we have prepared and consecrated; and behold, they are before the altar of the Lord."

This two-sided process must also be true of believers. If the sanctification of the Temple meant more than a few words to that effect, but active involvement in the process of total cleansing from impurity, so we, the present temples (naos) of God (1 Corinthians 3:16; 6:19, 20; 2 Corinthians 6:16) must be cleansed, made holy, to be truly His.[2] This is what sanctification ultimately means--holiness! The Greek word hagiasmos occurs ten times in the New Testament. The King James translates it as "holiness" five times

(Romans 6:19, 22; 1 Thessalonians 4:7; 1 Timothy 2:15; Hebrews 12:14) and five times as "sanctification" (1 Corinthians 1:30; 1 Thessalonians 4:3, 4; 2 Thessalonians 2:13; 1 Peter 1:2). The New American Standard Bible translates each reference with "sanctification" except 1 Timothy 2:15 as "sanctity" and 1 Peter 1:2 with "sanctifying," though the original American Standard Version of 1901 used "sanctification" throughout. There are other Greek words from the same basic root used in the New Testament with similar denotations of holiness and/or sanctification. A word study is not needed at this point. That sanctification is equivalent to holiness, however, is manifest by its primary meaning of being "set apart"--to God and from the world. We see this graphically in the verses preceding the verses alluding to our bodies as God's present temple in 1 Corinthians 6:9-11:

> Or do you not know that the unrighteous shall not inherit the kingdom of God? Do not be deceived neither fornicators, nor idolaters; nor adulterers, nor effeminate, nor homosexuals, nor thieves, nor the covetous, nor drunkards, nor revilers, nor swindlers, shall inherit the kingdom of God. And such were some of you; but you were washed, but you were sanctified, but you were justified in the name of the Lord Jesus Christ, and in the spirit of our God.

Discussions of sanctification and holiness usually lead to the questions of Christian sinlessness or perfectionism and eternal security. Thus some assert that if all the sins in the previous verses are past experiences, and sanctification means holiness, then surely the Christian must eventually arrive at a state of sinlessness.[3] If not, and sin remains a constant problem, then does not one lose the salvation he once had? On the other hand, others argue that if salvation is by the power of God, then surely one's sins cannot break the bond of salvation, and thus "once saved, always saved," regardless of the progress of sanctification and the state of one's holiness.

These two facets of salvation, progress in holiness and eternal security, have frequently been pitted against one another by the two primary camps of

137

Protestant theologians--Arminians and Calvinists. Though the debate may be more theoretical than practical, it does cause despair of lostness in some Arminian believers and the equally deep despair of sinfulness in some Calvinist oriented Christians. While the former question the continuance of their salvation, the latter question the joy and peace of their salvation. Neither live a so-called victorious Christian life. Students of either persuasion have their difficulties. Those from more Arminian churches frequently worry about their own or another's salvation due to the ever present power of sin and question the reality of eternal security. Those from more Calvinist settings, be they Reformed or Baptist oriented, may grow rather apathetic in regard to personal holiness as an evidence of God's work in their lives by relying instead on their baptism and/or church membership, or by recalling an "experience" of salvation rather than the fruits of holiness. Biblical balance, however, stresses that those who are practicing holiness are eternally secure and those who are eternally secure are living a life of holiness as an imperative of Christ's Lordship.

If sinless perfectionism is ruled out, what is the cause or condition that permits sin to always be a possibility in the life of the regenerated believer? This is usually attributed to the continual presence of the sin nature, or "old man" (Colossians 3:9, 10), that plagues us until we receive the resurrected and glorified body in heaven. Paul's testimony in Romans 7:18-23 is usually understood as indicating the continued possibility and problem of sin in the believer's life:

> For I know that nothing good dwells in me, that is, in my flesh; for the wishing is present in me, but the doing the good is not. For the good that I wish, I do not do; but I practice the very evil that I do not wish. But if I am doing the very thing I do not wish, I am no longer the one doing it, but sin which dwells in me. I find then the principle that evil is present in me, the one who wishes to do good. For I joyfully concur with the law of God in the inner man, but I see a different law in the members of my body, waging war against the law of my mind and

138

making me a prisoner of the law of
sin which is in my members.

Unless one understands this testimony as Paul's
reference to his spiritual life prior to the Damascus
Road encounter with the living Christ, which seems
impossible in light of his use of the present tense, it
must refer to his on-going battle with sinful propensities, and perhaps even habits, as a regenerated
Christian, yea even as an apostle. But to speak of an
"old nature" as if regeneration has not occurred seems
to present theological problems. Is the believer
really "new" in Christ and yet "old" in Satan? Is
there a constant division in the very structure of the
believer's essence or nature? This passage in Romans
would seem to answer "Yes!" Paul states that the
principle of "evil is present in me" (verse 21). But
at the same time, Paul also writes the very optimistic
and positive instruction in Romans 6:10-13:

> For the death that He [Christ]
> died, He died to sin, once for all;
> but the life that He lives, He
> lives to God. Even so consider
> yourselves to be dead to sin, but
> alive to God in Christ Jesus.
> Therefore do not let sin reign in
> your mortal body that you should
> obey its lusts, and do not go on
> presenting the members of your body
> to sin as instruments of unright-
> eousness; but present yourselves to
> God as those alive from the dead,
> and your members as instruments of
> righteousness to God.

How should these two passages in Romans 6 and 7 be
understood? Romans 7 seems to be pessimistic as to the
possibilities of ever defeating sin in one's on-going
experiences; Romans 6 gives us definite instruction to
be Christ-like and cease from allowing sin to control
us. The former assures us that sin will always be a
possibility as it will never be totally absent from our
body (7:23); at the same time, the latter passage,
Romans 6, definitely tells us that we need not allow
this ever-present sin to dominate or control us.

What is the difference, then, between these
seemingly contradictory passages? The answer is death!
Both chapters 6 and 7 begin with an illustration in

139

regard to the effects of death (see also Colossians 3:5). In chapter 6 Paul asks "how shall we who died to sin still live in it?" (verse 2). When did we die to sin? We died when we were identified with Christ and therefore identified with His substitutionary death for and on behalf of our sin (1 Peter 2:24; 3:18). Paul writes that "we have been buried with Him through baptism into death, in order that as Christ was raised from the dead through the glory of the Father, so we too might walk in newness of life" (Romans 6:4). Thus we are not only identified with Christ in death, but also in His resurrection and the power of a new life. We can, therefore, consider ourselves "to be dead to sin, but alive unto God." Our status in relation to the power of sin is absolutely different. While we once were "alive unto sin and dead" to the powerful and spiritual influence of God (Romans 8:5-8), it is now the exact opposite! We may now be "slaves of righteousness" because we have "been freed from sin" (Romans 6:18). We may "now present [our] members as slaves to righteousness, resulting in sanctification" (Romans 6:19; see also Galatians 5:16, 17). We can now consider ourselves to be dead to sin and alive unto holiness by the resurrection power of Christ that provides an entire new life--power, principle, purpose --a regeneration. For we now know "that our old self was crucified with Him that our body of sin might be done away with, that we should no longer be slaves to sin"! (Romans 6:6).

Chapter 7 also relates the effects of physical death to the realities of being identified with the death of Christ. Just as a woman is released from her husband by his death according to the Mosaic Law, and by no other way, and being so freed may marry another, so we "also were made to die to the Law, through the body of Christ, that [we] might be joined to another, to Him Who was raised from the dead, that we might bear fruit for God" (Romans 7:4). In other words, the power of sin is dead to us. We need not be slaves to sin. Christ has not only paid the penalty of sin but has also broken the power of sin for everyone who is identified with Him. Paul writes in Romans 8:10 that "if Christ is in you, though the body is dead because of sin, yet the spirit is alive because of righteousness." This means the truly regenerated person must be able to defeat sin and be victorious over Satan. If he cannot, then he is not one of His. Holiness is not only a distinct possibility for the believer but an expectation in that those joined to Him are to "bear fruit for God." No believer can escape the demand of Leviticus 11:44 and reiterated in 1 Peter 1:16: "YOU SHALL BE HOLY, FOR I AM HOLY."

This is not an affirmation of sinless perfectionism, however. Paul does not assert that sin and its potential is totally obliterated from our existence. He simply asserts that we are not to "let sin reign in [our] mortal bodies." In other words, sin is still present. My own pastor frequently asks "where do we live?" To which we are to answer, "we are still on earth." We are still in our mortal bodies. We are not yet absent from the presence of sin, not only before our eyes and ears, but from within our own egocentric impulses and habits. Paul well knows that sin still "dwells in me" and I find "the principle that evil is present in me." I can be holy, but I still may sin. Hebrews 12:10 tells us that God "disciplines us for our good that we may share his holiness." Obviously, then, both sin and holiness can reside in the same Christian individual during his life "on earth." I shall become more Christ-like, but I will not be conformed to His sinless image until I am removed from the presence of sin in my body when it is transformed from its present "humble state into conformity with the body of His glory" (Philippians 3:21). Meanwhile, we must consciously and willfully consider ourselves "to be dead to sin" through the enablement and power of the indwelling Holy Spirit and therefore lay "aside the old self with its evil practices" and "put on the new self who is being renewed to a true knowledge according to the image of the One who created him" (Colossians 3:9, 10; see also Romans 6:17-19). It should be noted that Paul speaks of the new self as "being renewed" (anakainoumenon), or in process of continuous renovation and spiritual growth. This is congruent with Peter's command to "grow in the knowledge of our Lord and Savior Jesus Christ" (2 Peter 3:18) so that we may "become partakers of the divine nature" (2 Peter 1:4). The renovation is not complete, however. Our bodies are still capable of any and all sins, but we also now, with Paul, may pray individually that "I may know Him, and the power of His resurrection and the fellowship of His sufferings, being conformed to His death" (Philippians 3:10). The two keys are again evident—Christ's death to sin and His resurrection power over sin unto newness of life.

There is yet one unanswered question as to the essence or structure of our new being after regeneration. Do we still have the old nature? Is the old fallen nature every bit as real, if not as powerful, as it was prior to salvation? Or is the old self, the sin nature, dead, and we are now each only a new, regenerated self? In Colossians 3 the tense of the verbs which Paul uses for "putting off" and "putting on" would seem to indicate a point in time in which the old self died and the new self was put on in regeneration. If this is a denial of an actual sinful nature residing in the believer, it does not give new credence to the doctrine of perfectionism. Paul very definitely sees that we are still in our bodies, the flesh, and that the members of our body may still be presented "as instruments of unrighteousness to God" (Romans 6:13). In a similar manner, Paul seems to separate his selfhood from the outworking of sin through his fleshly body members in chapter 7 of Romans. He speaks of "not practicing what I would like to do, but I am doing the very thing I hate" (verse 15) [italics added]. The "I" is separate from the consequences and habits of the flesh. He says the same thing in verses 17 and 18 when he writes: "So now, no longer am I the one doing it, but sin which indwells me. For I know that nothing good dwells in me, that is, in my flesh; for the wishing is present in me, but the doing of the good is not" [italics added]. Again there is a separation of his selfhood from his flesh. This, of course, is not true for the unbeliever. He wills to sin. He has no choice since he has only a fallen nature (Romans 8:7). But the believer in Christ is "a new creature; the old things passed away; behold, new things have come" (2 Corinthians 5:17). This total newness of his essential being is what Paul reflects in Romans 7:20, even if sin still is resident within his body members: "But if I am doing the very thing I do not wish, I am no longer the one doing it, but sin which dwells in me" [italics added].

The question of a resident sin nature in the believer, or the remnants of the flesh, the body, which is still to be redeemed, may be of more academic and theological interest than of benefit to our spiritual life in the process of sanctification. Whichever position we take, we are still capable of sin and have a battle with sin, though both perspectives believe that the saved individual can have success over the power and presence of sin. Those who understand sin as resident in our fleshly body and not our selfhood appear to have a problem with the willful sinfulness that is evidenced by believers? Is there no ultimate source or essence for the characteristics of sin that are manifested? On the other hand, those who understand that believers still have a sin nature seem to deny the absolute newness and all encompassing work of regeneration. In both cases, man is saddled with a sin nature, or the flesh, until the resurrection of the body. Until then, "we must press on toward the goal for the prize of the upward call of God in Christ Jesus" (Philippians 3:14).

Two things are now established: the believer will never be perfectly sinless, but neither is that an excuse for his lack of holiness. But we have one more facet to discuss briefly. Is the believer eternally secure? Is his <u>attaining</u> the goal "for the prize of the upward call of God in Christ Jesus" ever in doubt? Does the degree of progress in the process of sanctification determine one's eternal salvation? Or is the process assured? Many denominations have been spawned by different answers to these questions. The problem resides in missing one-or-the-other side of the coin by our myopic transfixion on only one side. We have seen that the finished work of Christ and the enablement of the Holy Spirit both free us from the power of sin and demand, while ensuring, a life of greater holiness during the process of sanctification. In an identical fashion, the same two gifts of God's love and grace ensure and secure the believer who has truly placed His faith in the finished work of the ascended Christ and experienced once-and-for-all the indwelling presence of the Holy Spirit.

It is Christ's finished work on Calvary and the work of the Holy Spirit in the true believer's life, both positionally and experientially, that makes one eternally secure. First Corinthians 6:19, 20 reminds us that we are not our own for we "have been bought with a price." We now belong to God. We are eternally secure in the Father's hand (John 10:29). Paul was absolutely sure that what God had begun in us--new life--He was able to complete (Romans 4:21; Philippians 1:6; 2 Timothy 1:12).

This new life is "not of seed which is perishable, but imperishable" (1 Peter 1:23). It is God's work. The very meaning of regeneration (<u>paliggenesia</u>) is "born again." We are now made new (2 Corinthians 5:17; Colossians 3:9-11). The new life we receive in regeneration is the life of Christ in resurrection (Ephesians 2:6; Colossians 2:12). We are, therefore, declared righteous, justified, and have peace with God (Romans 5:1). We cannot be made guilty and hell-bound again. God's wrath is no longer upon our "ungodliness and unrighteousness." There is a new standing and a new being before God. We cannot be disowned as sons! Our new nature in Christ is as immutable as the physical nature we inherit at physical birth. Since we are now "in Christ," there is "now no condemnation" (Romans 8:1; see also vss. 33-38). We now "may have confidence in the day of judgment; because as He is, so also are we in this world" (1 John 4:17). Judgment is passed for Christ and those truly associated with His resurrection through faith. Therefore the believer has confidence for he is as eternally secure as His Lord. On the other hand, to deny eternal security for the believer who partakes in both Christ's substitutionary death and resurrection life is either to deny the once-for-all nature of His death and the reality of His life or to deny their imperishable and everlasting character for the individual believer. Is not the latter option as distasteful as the former in light of God's infinite love, omnipotent power, and truthful Word? Can the finite creature really undo the work and will of the infinite and holy God?

In addition to Christ's finished work, resurrection life, and present intercession on behalf of His children (John 17:1-26; Romans 8:34; Hebrews 7:23-25; 1 John 2:1, 2), there is the reality of the Holy Spirit's ministry on behalf of and in the true believer. In 1 Corinthians 12:13 we read that "by one Spirit we were baptized into one body, whether Jews or Greeks, whether slaves or free, and we were all made to drink of one Spirit." The primary context of this much disputed verse is the Pauline illustration of the union of the members of the body with the head of the body. As he says in the following verse, "the body is not one member, but many" (1 Corinthians 12:14). It is also very important to note that Paul envisions, in light of the tense he chose for the key word "baptism" (ebaptisthemen), that this was the experience of every Corinthian believer, carnal or spiritual, at some point in the past. The only common point in their spiritual past was their regeneration. This baptism of the Holy Spirit is the operation of God's Spirit by which the Christian is brought into organic union with Christ's spiritual body--the Church. The Christian is placed into the body of Christ, be he Jew or Gentile, at the time of his salvation (Ephesians 2:13-16). This is his eternal abode--in Christ. He now shares in God's

144

righteousness by being a member of Christ's body. But what must be noted for our immediate purposes is that there will be no amputated members of Christ's body. This is the very point of the entire passage (2 Corinthians 12:13-27). Each is indispensable and no one will be lost. There was a fall in the first Adam, but there is no fall from the Second Adam! As all are damned in the first Adam, so all who believe are eternally safe in the Second Adam (Romans 5:17).

Closely associated with the baptism of the Holy Spirit is His work of sealing and indwelling the believer. In fact, He Himself is the seal! We read in Ephesians 1:13, 14:

> In Him, you also, after listening to the message of truth, the gospel of your salvation--having also believed, you were sealed in Him with the Holy Spirit of promise, who is given as a pledge of our inheritance, with a view to the redemption of God's own possession, to the praise of His glory.

We again must note that the key word, "sealed" (esphragisthete), is in the same tense as the word "baptism" in 1 Corinthians 12:13. Therefore, the time of the sealing must be concomitant and simultaneous with the believer's regeneration and baptism. Paul sees both the Spirit's baptism and sealing as past events in the lives of the believers to whom he is writing. At the same time that the Spirit's baptism places us in the body of Christ, the Holy Spirit becomes the very seal of ownership and authentication until "the day of redemption" (Ephesians 4:30). The Holy Spirit is apparently seen as both the sealer and seal in the Ephesians passages since they can be translated as "sealed in," or "sealed by," or "sealed with" the Holy Spirit. There does not seem to be any problem in accepting that He is both sealer and seal instead of quibbling over one or the other of these. The Holy Spirit seals the believer into the body of Christ by the baptism of the Holy Spirit and becomes the seal of ownership by the very indwelling presence in the believer. The biblical significance of the Holy Spirit as the seal via indwelling is seen in 1 Corinthians 6:19, 20--ownership! This is the mark by which "The Lord knows those who are His" (2 Timothy 2:19).

145

The Holy Spirit not only is God's mark of identification, but also His promise to us that our salvation will be completed by the redemption of our mortal body. Paul states this clearly in 2 Corinthians 5:4-6. The Spirit is given to us "as a pledge" that, though we are now "at home in the body" and therefore "absent from the Lord," our mortal bodies will yet "be swallowed up by life." This identification of the Holy Spirit's personal indwelling of every individual believer with His sealing is unambiguously stated by Paul when he writes:

> Now He who establishes us with you
> in Christ and anointed us is God,
> who also sealed us and gave us the
> Spirit in our hearts as a pledge
> (2 Corinthians 1:21, 22).

This word "pledge" (arrabon) is used only in these passages in 2 Corinthians and Ephesians 1:14. It was a common word in the economic and cultural life of that era signifying a down payment, or earnest money, as a pledge of full payment for the purchase of an expensive item, or as a partial payment of a dowry for a wife. This "down payment" of the Holy Spirit in the believer's heart is both God's sign of ownership and a "pledge of our inheritance, with a view to the redemption of God's own possession" (Ephesians 1:14). A clearer indication of the believer's eternal security could hardly be requested. We are God's and He has assured us of such by the indwelling of Himself within us. Only those who have the Holy Spirit are God's (Romans 8:9), and God will not in effect lie by reneging on His promise of bringing us to the day of complete redemption (Ephesians 4:30) and completing the good work He has begun in us (Philippians 1:6). God Himself is our pledged security even as He is our provided redemption.

Eternal security cannot be denied, therefore, on the basis of God's work in the Persons of Jesus Christ and the Holy Spirit. Eternal security is not a matter of our will power or faith, but God's deliverance and promise. If God justifies us, then who is left that can really condemn us? If Christ has paid the penalty for our sin, and made us to be partakers of His resurrected life, then who or what can separate us from the love of God? If God has provided us a pledge of His intentions for those who are in Christ, then who or what can interfere with the purposes and plans of God?

The answer to these questions is obvious. Therefore we are kept by God's word and power not our own good intentions and willfulness. This does not mean that we may "continue in sin that grace might increase" for "how shall we who died to sin still live in it?" (Romans 6:1, 2). Rather, new birth demands a new quality of life. Hebrews 12:14 informs us that without sanctification (holiness) "no one will see the Lord." The reverse side of eternal security is holiness and vice versa. No one can make claims to one without receiving full-title to the other. They cannot be separated by logic nor convenience. Just as Christ is not an adequate Redeemer without being both divine and human, so there are no true Christians who are not both holy and eternally secure!

> If then you have been raised up with Christ, keep seeking the things above, where Christ is, seated at the right hand of God. Set your mind on the things above, not on things that are on the earth. For you have died and your life is hidden with Christ in God. When Christ, who is our life is revealed, then you also will be revealed with Him in glory (Colossians 3:1-4).

1. Define sanctification. How is it a two-sided process? Why have Arminians and Calvinists usually divided over emphasis on holiness and eternal security?

2. Compare and contrast the optimism of Romans 6 with the pessimism of Romans 7. Why must both passages be descriptive of the believer's experience? Are these passages ultimately compatible?

3. What is meant by an "old" or "sin" nature? Discuss this nature in the context of 2 Corinthians 5:17 and Colossians 3:9, 10.

4. If the believer does <u>not</u> have an old nature, does this mean sinless perfectionism is within our grasp? If not, why not? If this is the case, is the conflict between Romans 6 and 7 more reconcilable? Explain, in some detail, either answer.

5. What are the two foundational facts in regard to the doctrine of eternal security? Is this doctrine inherently antinomian?

6. Discuss eternal security and regeneration. Why can these two doctrines not be separated? Of what significance is the death and resurrection of Christ for the believer's eternal security?

7. Identify and distinguish between the baptism and indwelling of the Holy Spirit? How is eternal security inherently implied in these biblical teachings? What is the significance of being sealed "by" and "with" the Holy Spirit for the believer's eternal security?

ENDNOTES

[1]A helpful introductory article is Philip Edgcumbe Hughes, "Sanctify, Sanctification," _Dictionary of Theology_, edited by Everett F. Harrison (Grand Rapids: Baker Book House, 1960), pp. 470, 471.

[2]It is interesting to note that the word translated temple (_naos_) in both 1 Corinthians 3:16 and 6:19 is really the word for God's sanctuary, His dwelling-place, the holy of holies. If that is what "we are" through the indwelling presence of the Holy Spirit, it is no wonder that holiness is an absolute demand. See A. T. Robertson, _Word Pictures in the New Testament_, six volumes (Nashville: Broadman Press, 1931), IV, 98.

[3]Those who believe in sinless perfectionism usually redefine sin, narrowing its conception. John Wesley is reported to have said: "I believe a person filled with love of God is still liable to involuntary transgressions. Such transgressions you may call sins, if you please; I do not."

CHAPTER XII

CHURCH: BOTH PROCLAMATION AND CHARITY

> Go therefore and make disciples of
> all the nations, baptizing them in
> the name of the Father and the Son
> and the Holy Spirit, teaching them
> to observe all that I commanded
> you; and lo, I am with you always,
> even to the end of the age (Matthew
> 28:19, 20).

> And whoever in the name of a
> disciple gives to one of these
> little ones even a cup of cold
> water to drink, truly I say to you
> he shall not lose his reward
> (Matthew 10:42).

These two verses in Matthew express the twin
obligations of Christ's Lordship upon the individual
Christian and collectively upon the body of Christ and
its expression through local churches. During the
twentieth century these dual obligations of Christ's
Lordship have been practically discarded by many.[1] The
liberal wing of Christianity, usually with no transcendent message of salvation to offer, reduces Christianity to Christian charity that differs little from
humanistic care for the needy and disadvantaged. This
so-called "social gospel" was developed by caring
theologians and pastors at the turn of the century.[2]
From one perspective, it was needed. The masses of
immigrants pouring into our cities during the 1890s and
1900s provided hands and muscle for industry, but
little personal respect for these people as individuals
made in God's image. Frequently, however, their
adjustment and physical needs were alone recognized to
the neglect of their spiritual needs before a holy God.
Subsequently, when the modernist-fundamentalist
controversy broke out in many denominations in the
1920s, those with a true sin-delivering proclamation so
separated themselves from the social gospelers that
they forgot or neglected the gospel's obligation of
Christian charity and Christian proclamation.

Both dimensions of the gospel must be proclaimed
and practiced by the Church. Jesus certainly proclaimed the centrality of His Person and mission when
he stated to Zaccheus that "salvation has come to this

house" for He, the Son of Man, had "come to seek and to save that which was lost" (Luke 19:9, 10). Man is lost and must be redeemed through the substitutionary atonement of our Lord. This is primary! However, we also read that Jesus had "compassion" on lepers, the blind and deaf, and others with physical problems. In Matthew 15:30 we read that "the multitudes came to Him, bringing with them those who were lame, crippled, blind, dumb, and many others, and they laid them down at His feet; and he healed them." Jesus' works were works of empathy and charity as well as signs and wonders of His identity (Matthew 11:2-6; John 10:37, 38). This is why Peter not only claims to the Jews assembled at Pentecost that Jesus was "a man attested to you by God with miracles and wonders and signs," but at Cornelius' house also announces that God had "anointed Him with the Holy Spirit and with power, and how He went about doing good, and healing all who were oppressed by the devil" (Acts 2:22; 10:38) [italics added].

Jesus' mode of ministry must be the Church's model of ministry. Man is not either spirit or body, but both! Protestant liberalism frequently practices charity as if it had a naturalistic view of man. Certainly, men, women, and children must be physically cared for. Starving individuals must be fed because they are fellow-creatures made by God with distinct dignity and worth. Medicines that easily cure or control various diseases must be shared and taken to the undeveloped and poor third-world nations. North/South international dialogue must come between the rich and poor nations, the have and have-not individuals. But this is not the gospel of Jesus Christ. Humanistic concern totally detached from Christianity can care for our bodies and developing brains, but what of our spirit? Although Jesus most certainly fed the hungry, and healed the blind and leprous, He also proclaimed to Satan himself that "man shall not live on bread alone, but on every word that proceeds out of the mouth of God" (Matthew 4:4).

The gospel, then, has to do also and more importantly, with man's eternal being. Not only are we physical creatures made to live in a real physical world with economic, political, and social concerns, but we are creatures made to fellowship with our Creator. Without restating emphases of previous chapters, man is separated from, and under the wrath of, God. The incarnation of God's Son was not for the

152

purpose of economic equality or social justice. Rather, as Paul wrote Timothy, "Christ Jesus came into the world to save sinners, among whom I am foremost of all" (1 Timothy 1:15). This is the universal message needed by rich and poor, educated and uneducated, healthy and sick, advantaged and disadvantaged. This is what missions is primarily about. Preachers must be primarily sent with and because of this universal and time-transcending message (Romans 10:14, 15). Salvation from the penalty, power, and eventually the presence of sin, is what the gospel, the church, and Christian mission are all about. It is only when one hears the proclamation that "God so loved the world, that He gave His only begotten Son, that whoever believes in Him should not perish, but have eternal life" (John 3:16) that an individual can "confess with [his] mouth Jesus as Lord, and believe in [his] heart that God raised Him from the dead" and thus be saved (Romans 10:9). It is only when we believe in our heart, the very essence and soul of our being, as well as confessing with our mouth, that we receive Christ's righteousness and salvation. This is the absolute essence and core of gospel proclamation at home or abroad.

However, we must not forget that the gospel comes to man as physical and social men. We are not eternal spirit only. We are body. We are individuals with different human needs that cannot be overlooked by eternity's prior values. Gospel proclamation by biblical Christians must not make the same, if opposite mistake, of social gospelers. Man is both spirit and body. Therefore, the gospel addresses man in our totality. While the eternal destiny of man is ultimately more important than his temporal problems, it is difficult if not impossible to hear eternal words in a body ravaged with pain or a brain undernourished and thus incapable of comprehending the redemption story. We cannot bifurcate man. We must recognize our integral being made from the dust of the ground and in God's image. We cannot be separated as to spirit and body, not even in eternity if we really take the doctrine of individual resurrection seriously (1 Corinthians 15:20-24, 42-57).

Ironically, conservative Christians have often practiced a more wholistic Christianity during the twentieth century on foreign mission fields than we have at home. There are very few Christians who question the building of hospitals and dispensatories,

if located in third-world countries, to meet the urgent
and pressing physical needs of countless thousands. At
times such work may be seen as only a means to an end--
evangelism. This is legitimate as one recognizes the
priority of the spirit, though it might be preferred
that food and medical assistance were offered not
simply as a means, but because of the absolute worth of
the human individual as an individual.

Nevertheless, such human needs are met by Christian missionaries of nearly every denomination.
However, with the exception of inner-city missions,
such concern for the physical and social needs of
fellow Americans is all too often labeled "social
gospel," causing the same churches that support this
type of activity abroad to withdraw from such endeavors
at home. This same label keeps good and capable
Christian men and women from becoming involved in civic
concerns, public school boards, local government, and
numerous other social engagements as individual
Christians. This nearly total withdrawal of biblical
Christianity from the spheres of influence in American
society during this past half-century has speeded the
growth of secularism at every level. The First
Amendment of our Constitution is now usually interpreted as meaning the state is to be totally free of
the influence of religious values rather than its
original intention of protecting the free expression of
religion against the threat of one National Church.
There is certainly no guarantee that the voice of
individual Christians in whatever culture or society
will halt the growth of secularism and moral decay.
But the quietness and passive acquiescence of the
German church during the 1930s should be warning enough
that, when Christians stand on the sidelines, others
will fill the vacuum with no concept of either the
absolute worth of the individual, or of the state ruled
by the cultural and historical expressions of God's
absolute Law. Francis Schaeffer has stated that there
are now only two alternatives for Western societies
(the United States most definitely included) which have
no ultimate foundation for right and wrong but only
various combinations of relative pragmatism and
utilitarianism: either "imposed order" or "our society
once again affirming that base which gives freedom
without chaos in the first place--God's revelation in
the Bible and his revelation through Christ."[3]

The purpose of this brief chapter is not to
promote political slogans nor societal involvement

simply for the sake of societal involvement. There is no historical warrant, let alone biblical mandate, for such activity as indispensable for the Christian believer simply in its own right. But there is a biblical mandate for both proclamation and charity. In John 17:18, our Lord's High Priestly prayer for His disciples of every age, He states:

> As Thou didst send Me into the world, I also have sent them into the world.

Obviously, we are not sent into the world in an identical fashion as Christ. He is the Anointed One, the Messiah, Immanuel, our Savior. But nevertheless we are sent as He was sent. Our absolute and primary task as His ambassadors is to proclaim the good news of redemption and salvation and beg men "on behalf of Christ, be reconciled to God" (2 Corinthians 5:20). This was the message of the apostles throughout the book of Acts. But at the same time many people were cared for and healed who had physical handicaps and social injustices were remedied such as the slave girl in Philippi (Acts 16:16-19). The apostles had the same sympathetic consciousness of others' distress and a desire to alleviate it as did their Lord. This is the compassion Jesus taught when He told the parable of the Good Samaritan (Luke 10:30-37).

The Good Samaritan story was told to an inquirer who asked "who is my neighbor" in reply to Jesus' admonition that the Law was fulfilled by loving "the Lord your God" with all your heart, soul, strength, and mind "and your neighbor as yourself" (Luke 10:27, 28). It is the hated Samaritan that provides bandages to the injured man and pays for his continued care, not the religious leaders of priest and Levite, or may we say, elder and deacon. It is the unbelieving, a rebel from Israel proper, that tends to the concerns that should be a priority of those who provide spiritual guidance and lead the worship of the called-out community. The initial inquirer has no difficulty in identifying the true neighbor, the real upholder of God's law, and is given the injunction to "go and do the same." Neither a preacher nor a writer need to elaborate on Christ's will for the Christian in a world much smaller when nearly everyone is "our neighbor"--"go and do the same."

Jesus taught by example as well as story. Only one such example is needed here to illustrate Jesus' compassion toward the outcasts of society. In Mark 1:40-45 is recorded an incident with a leper that doubtless helped bring Jesus to the attention of the people since Mark concludes his record of this event by writing that the people "were coming to Him from everywhere" (verse 45). The leper had heard of Jesus as he wandered outside the city walls, in the garbage heaps salvaging for food, and shouting "unclean, unclean" whenever a non-leper was at all close to his person. He certainly called to Jesus from at least some distance, but he called in faith: "If You are willing, You can make me clean." We read that Jesus, "moved with compassion," did that which no leper could ever expect. He probably took a few steps in his direction, and then "stretched out His hand and <u>touched</u> him, and said to him, 'I am willing; be cleansed,' and <u>immediately</u> the leprosy left him and he was cleansed" (verses 41, 42) [italics added]. This event in the life of Christ is recorded primarily as a sign of His Messiahship and as an analogy with the immediate manner in which a man can be cleansed from the leprosy of sin if he calls on Jesus as Christ and Lord in faith. Nevertheless, it also illustrates Jesus' love and attention to mankind's physical ills. It is a demonstration of His care and personal concern as He <u>touched</u> the leper. He did not need to do that to heal him. But He did need to do that to provide a lesson to His disciples that we do not minister at a physical and social distance, nor do we treat those less-fortunate than ourselves with unChrist-like disdain by making them "keep their distance" and/or "know their place." We are not only one as fellow-humans (Acts 17:26), but we may be "brothers in Christ" regardless of skin pigmentation, developmental disabilities, chronic illness, cultural diversity, social stratification, or vocational choices. All of these, and more, make artificial divisions in the Christian community that drowns out the proclamation by a sea of bitterness, hatred, and resentment rather than Christian charity and love. Paul implemented such charity and brotherhood when he instructed Philemon to receive Onesimus not as a slave, but "a beloved brother," putting whatever debt that might be outstanding to Paul's account (Philemon 1:16, 18).

The early Christian church attempted to deal with the problems of social and economic differences by having "all things in common" (Acts 2:44). This apparent communalism was an attempt to enhance Christian brotherhood by the voluntary sharing of one's wealth with others. The Ananias and Sapphira debacle (Acts 5:1-11) probably marked at least the beginning of the end to the initial thrust toward communalism in the early church since no continuing directions and instructions are provided in the Epistles. But certainly the sharing of what we have is not only continued but commanded, both explicitly and implicitly. John writes that "if someone says, 'I love God,' and hates his brother, he is a liar; for the one who does not love his brother whom he has seen, cannot love God whom he has not seen" (1 John 4:20). Some may contend that such sharing as John here seemingly has in mind applies only to our fellow-Christians. This may be so, for we certainly have a need of much greater charity toward other Christians, and especially those who are mentally and physically handicapped, educationally disadvantaged, temporarily unemployed, and culturally diverse. This lack has often caused resentment, or even deafness, to biblical proclamation within the community of faith. James knew this could be the case when he wrote that Christians must demonstrate their faith by their works (James 2:18). James stressed that while saving faith was by the heart, we could not neglect the bodily needs of others. His explicit statement is its own best commentary as to the absolute prerequisite of both proclamation and charity:

> If a brother or sister is without
> clothing and in need of daily food,
> and one of you says to them, "Go in
> peace, be warmed and be filled,"
> and yet you do not give them what
> is necessary for their body, what
> use is that (James 2:15, 16)
> [italics added].

The early church thus realized the fact through conscious practice that they were sent "into the world" even as their Lord. Proclamation was primary, charity was indispensable. There could not be the former in a true biblical manner without the latter. People were whole beings, body and spirit. The love of God in Christ extended to the whole man. There was no twentieth century perversion of the gospel as only proclamation or only charity. The gospel first and foremost was intended to reconcile sinful men with a holy God through Christ. But the gospel also addresses

157

itself to all areas of life--physical, social, economic, political--or there is no such thing as a Christian world view. Individual salvation must have an effect on a society's quality of life or we have a right to question its vitality. Paul knew this as he gave inspired ethical instruction in social-cultural dress in 1 Corinthians, especially chapter 9, or as he offered a perspective toward even a pagan state in Romans 13:1-7.

Times have changed since the first century. The same absolute ethical principles, however, must be applied to problems of a different historical era and to numerous social-cultural environments. But applied they must be! Opportunity for being an agent of change within one's nation is greatly different today in democratic states from the opportunities offered first-century Christians in a Roman state. The Roman Empire not only disfranchised the vast majority of her people, but the definition of good citizenship for those who were not disfranchised was passivity and acceptance of the status quo. There were few means to agitate for change or to Christianly address the issues of the day. Though it may have been the case, however, that the hope to influence the citadel of power may have been a part of Paul's desire to see Rome.

This is not the case today. Western democracies, especially America, provide us the opportunity and privilege to make known biblical principles, regardless of the reaction of the mass-media. The abortion issue, to list one of many, is an example where God's perspective toward the inherent worth of every baby made in His image must challenge the secular and humanistic status quo. The church as church cannot be "en bloc" a political machine. The church as concerned Christian believers must be socially and politically involved if we are to be in but not of our contemporary world (John 17:11, 14). This is, of course, impossible in many states and thus Christian charity will be expressed in patterns very similar to the first century. American Christians, however, cannot decry the loss of a Christian consensus in our country during the twentieth century when we have been on the sidelines since the end of the first quarter. Francis Schaeffer tried to awaken the conservative Christian community to our responsibilities as Christian citizens in a state that still permits our active, if now attenuated, voice in the affairs of nation and state.[4] This too is really Christian clarity! Christian charity is not simply

158

direct monetary and tangible help to those in economic need and physical stress. It is also charitable to attempt to uphold God's absolute law above human relative law for the possibilities of a just society. Biblical history amply provides evidence of the blessings or judgments of God depending upon the religious interest and ethical values of the ruling officials. More evidence is provided if we simply contrast the opportunities of freedom and justice between the United States and Soviet Russia, or between, say, Great Britain and Poland. This is not to say that either of these Western nations are really Christian today or yesterday. It is to say that the freedom and greater attempts at economic, legal, and social justice in these countries is due to the much greater Christian consensus and involvement of biblical Christians in the seats of authority and influence in the past. Christian charity, then does not stop, but only begins, with our immediate neighbors. Nor is it exhausted by providing food, housing, clothing and other necessities out of and on behalf of the love of Christ. Christian charity is also attempting to influence one's society (to the extent possible) with the Christian ethic based on the absolute Word of God in Holy Scripture. Christian ethics is thus both a proclamation of Christ and a projected pattern of Christ-like charity in a watching world that is controlled by the duplicity of the present but temporary prince of this world. Only by both proclamation and charity can individual believers as well as the community of truth and love, the Christian church, be the "salt of the earth" and the "light of the world" (Matthew 5:13, 14). Men do love "darkness rather than the light" because of their evil deeds (John 3:19), but the light of proclaimed truth can penetrate the darkness of any culture to the glory of God and the salvation of those who come to that light (John 3:21; Romans 10:8-17). Likewise, Christians as salt not only give the tastiness of charity but the preservative of truth. But salt is ineffective in either role if it remains in the salt-shaker rather than being applied to, in, and with the food. In an identical fashion, with no necessary compromise of tastiness or preservative powers, Christians can be be the "salt of the world" only by being in the world but not of the world because they are sent into the world by a New Master (John 17:23), their Savior, the coming Christ of glory and hope, with a New Word (John 17:8), and a New Love (John 17:26) provided by their Master and Lord for the purposes of both proclamation and charity.

REFLECTION

1. Why must both biblical proclamation and Christian charity be undertaken by the Christian Church? What has caused these to be separated by many churches during the twentieth century?

2. Which of the above must have priority? Does this permit the heretical exclusion of the other dimension? Discuss the dynamics of this latter phenomena. In what way are foreign missionary policies frequently different from local church practices? Can this be justified?

3. Why is Luke 19:13 and John 17:18 so important for Christian witness? Is such witness simply evangelistic testimony? May biblical Christians be partially at fault for the growing secularism in our culture by so narrowly defining their moral responsibilities and societal roles?

4. Discuss the parable of the Good Samaritan (Luke 10:30-37). What is the immediate context that prompts this story? Why must this parable be taken to heart by twentieth century conservative Christianity?

5. What can we learn from the practice of Jesus in Mark 1:40-45? Do believers, like unbelievers, create artificial walls of separation between individuals?

6. How did the early church attempt to deal with the problems of social and economic differences? Was it successful? If not, what caused it to fail? What biblical principle still remains? Is James 2:15, 16 still applicable?

7. Discuss the different conception of citizenship between the Roman Empire and twentieth century democracies. Does this change the scope of the individual believer's witness? How may we understand Matthew 5:13, 14 in the context of contemporary society? Is Christian charity more than tangible assistance to those in need? If so, why is Christian charity, broadly defined, indispensable to gospel proclamation?

[1]That this was absolutely not the case in nineteenth century America where, for instance, Christians were among the most effective advocates of abolitionism, see Timothy Smith, <u>Revivalism and Social Reform</u> (New York: Harper Torchbooks, 1957) and Louis Filler, <u>The Crusade Against Slavery</u> (New York: Harper Torchbooks, 1960).

[2]Leading advocates were pastors such as Washington Gladden and the Baptist theologian Walter Rauschenbusch. Their writings were the religious backbone of the early twentieth century drive for social and economic justice. See Washington Gladden, <u>The Church and Modern Life</u> (Boston: Houghton Mifflin and Company, 1908) and Walter Rauschenbusch, <u>Christianity and the Social Crisis</u> (New York: The Macmillan Company, 1907) and <u>A Theology of the Social Gospel</u> (New York: Abingdon, 1917).

[3]Francis Schaeffer, <u>How Should We Then Live</u> (Old Tappan, New Jersey: Fleming H. Revell Company, 1976), p. 252. This same lack of an ultimate foundation for human rights, even at the International Institute of Human Rights, University of Strasbourg, France, which I attended during the summer of 1981, is the reason John Warwick Montgomery conducts a Seminary on Theology and Law simultaneously with the Institute.

[4]See in particular his book, <u>A Christian Manifesto</u> (Westchester, Illinois: Crossway Books, 1981).

CHAPTER XIII

LAST THINGS: BOTH ALREADY AND NOT YET

One of the major disagreements among doctrinally conservative Christians is the debate over what are usually called "last things." Last things for both groups means the resurrection of the saints, the final judgment, and the culmination of all things. But have the "last times" already begun? For those of a more Reformed perspective the answer is a very definite "Yes!" The book of Revelation is usually interpreted in a historical or symbolic manner rather than a more literal fashion which understands the descriptions of the book of Revelation as future, historical judgments of the "last days" to be followed by the literal rule of Christ for 1,000 years, or the Millennium. For Reformed Christians, however, the millennial passages are understood either as the present rule of God in the hearts and lives of His saints, or as figurative descriptions of the eternal state. The Church is understood as the new Israel of God, transferring the physical and tangible promises to the nation into spiritual and intangible blessings in the body of Christ. This transaction was initiated by Jesus Christ announcing the present reality of the kingdom of God in our hearts (Matthew 12:28; 13:24-30).[1] Those who affirm a literal kingdom of the millennium frequently deny any present reality of the kingdom of God and stress the absolute distinction of the nation Israel and the Church.[2] The intent of this final chapter is to sketch briefly the truth of both positions. That is, while Israel and the Church are not identical, there is a very distinctive sense in which the kingdom of God has both come and we still await it. (Remember the argument of the New Covenant in chapter 9.) Thus one need not say that the kingdom is present with us and therefore there is no future historical and literal manifestation of such, any more than one need deny the present aspect of the kingdom to maintain a literal 1,000 year reign of Christ in the future.

This position may be called the "already and the not yet." The theological phraseology originated with Oscar Cullmann, the French New Testament scholar, but the concept is totally biblical.[3] The final revelation of God, and the mid-point of history from a biblical perspective, is the incarnation of Jesus, the Christ. Hebrews 1:1, 2 makes this clear: "God, after He spoke long ago to the fathers in the prophets in many portions and in many ways, in these <u>last days</u> has spoken to us in His Son, whom He appointed heir of all things, through whom also He made the world" [italics added]. This enfleshment of God in the midst of human history had been promised since the protevangelium of Genesis 3:15. This coming of the Messiah, Immanuel (Isaiah 7:14; 9:6), was seen by the prophets of Israel as dividing history into the time <u>before</u> the Messiah and the time <u>after</u> the Messiah, the latter being understood as the "last time." This Old Testament mentality can be observed in the way in which the Christianized Western world has adopted the practice of differentiating history into "before Christ" and "after Christ."[4] Christ is thus seen as the mid-point of history. Our practice of numbering both backward and forward from the birth of Christ is more than mere convenience. It "actually presupposes fundamental assertions of <u>New Testament theology</u> concerning time and history"[5] [original italics].

This can be seen by the chosen text and exposition of the first great sermon of Christianity--Peter's Pentecostal sermon. The commotion of hearing the apostles speak in "our own tongues" by people of many diverse places and different languages (Acts 2:8-10) provoked the misinterpretation that the prophets were drunk (Acts 2:13). Peter refuted this by noting the hour of the day (9 a.m.) and then pointed out that "this is what was spoken of through the prophet Joel" (Acts 2:16). What had Joel said?

> "And it shall be in the last days,"
>   God says,
> "That I will pour forth of My
>   Spirit upon all mankind;
> And your sons and your daughters
>   shall prophesy,
> And your young men shall see
>   visions,
> And your old men shall dream
>   dreams;
> Even upon My bondslaves, both men
>   and women,
> I will in those days pour forth of
>   My Spirit
> And they shall prophesy.
> And I will grant wonders in the sky
>   above,
> And signs on the earth beneath,

Blood, and fire, and vapor of
  smoke.
The sun shall be turned into
  darkness,
And the moon into blood,
Before the great and glorious day
  of the LORD shall come.
And it shall be that everyone who
  calls on the name of the LORD
  shall be saved" (Joel 2:28-
  32).

Peter definitely understands this outpouring of
the Holy Spirit and its accompanying ability to speak
in tongues as the fulfillment of Joel's prophecy
concerning the "last days." But why now? The answer
is that Jesus had been "exalted to the right hand of
God" since His resurrection, of which Peter and some
120 people were witnesses, and therefore the last times
have begun (Acts 2:32, 33). This most assuredly does
not mean that all that Joel predicted in these verses
was coming to pass at Pentecost, but that nevertheless
the last days had begun! The Holy Spirit is thus the
"Pledge" ("earnest," KJV) that all the Messianic
expectations and promises will be fulfilled (Romans
8:23; 2 Corinthians 1:22; 5:5). As the old but
excellent Bible expositor, F. E. Marsh writes, "the
Spirit as the Earnest is God's Pledge that He will keep
to all He has promised."[6] Or as Cullmann notes, "the
Holy Spirit is nothing else than the anticipation of
the end in the present."[7]

Peter is not alone in proclaiming that we are now
in the last days, or Messianic Age. John states the
same thing in regard to the numerous antichrists who
have appeared already. He writes in 1 John 2:18:

Children, it is the last hour; and
just as you heard that antichrist
is coming, even now many antichrists have arisen; from this we
know that it is the last hour.

Because the antichrists have appeared, John thus
argues, we know the last hour (literally "eschaton
era") has arrived. Notice two things: first it is the
last hour because the antichrists are here. The
antichrists are false teachers who deny or stand
against the Christ. John very probably had particular
men, for example Cerinthus, in mind. Nevertheless for

antichrists to appear, it was necessary that the Christ had previously appeared. Antichrists can only stand against that which has appeared already in history. It is the Christ, not the antichrists, that has really inaugurated the last hour. Secondly, John expressedly endorses the "already and not yet" facet of last things. While the antichrists have "already" appeared, the absolute and final historical manifestation of the sinfulness and autonomy of man "is coming." The Antichrist is "not yet"! There is yet future fulfillment and ramification. Lenski notes:

> John is not determining the duration of the "final hour," he is pointing his readers to the sign which indicates its beginning, the appearance of many antichrists: "whence we know (ginosko, with concern to ourselves) that it is (indeed) final hour." John saw the first group of antichrists. He distinguishes these from "Antichrist," of whom he does not say that he has already come to be but only that "he is coming" [original italics].[8]

Thus both the coming of the Holy Spirit, the believer's anointing (Romans 8:9, 1 John 2:20, 27), and the coming of the antichrists (the unanointed ones) who stand against Christ and His indwelt anointed ones, are signs that the eschaton era, the last time, is upon us (see also 1 John 4:1-4). It is not inaugurated by either of these however, but by the coming of the Christ Himself (Hebrews 1:1, 2). Peter knew this when he wrote that "Christ has appeared in these last times for the sake of you" (1 Peter 1:20). He is the midpoint of history. The Divider between the "before times" and the "last times." Nevertheless, both the Holy Spirit and the antichrists are the certain "pointers," positively and negatively, of the reality of the eschaton in the "already."

Peter and John are not alone in enunciating that the promised Messianic kingdom has already come. Their authority for comprehending the present era as the promised era of the Old Testament is Jesus' words:

> But if I cast out demons by the spirit of God, then the kingdom of

God has come upon you" (Matthew
12:28) [italics added].

Now having been questioned by the
Pharisees as to when the kingdom of
God was coming, He answered them
and said, "The kingdom of God is
not coming with signs to be
observed; nor will they say, 'Look,
here it is!' or, 'There it is!'
For behold the kingdom of God is in
your midst" (Luke 17:20, 21)
[italics added].

The kingdom dimension of which Jesus spoke in these
passages is obviously not physical, but it is real!
While one could not point to the geographical location
of the kingdom as the Pharisees anticipated, this did
not mean there was not a literal reality of God's
kingdom in the hearts of men. The apostles had the
same misunderstandings earlier, and they would again,
even after the resurrection. The Transfiguration
occurred to dispel the disciples' doubts and questions,
though it was not totally successful due to their
weariness of body and apparent hard-headedness as to
Messianic expectations. For just one week or so prior
to the Transfiguration, Jesus had asked His disciples
"who do the multitudes say that I am?" After various
answers, including Elijah and John the Baptist, Jesus
asked a second question, "But who do you say that I
am?" To which Peter immediately answered, "The Christ
of God" (Luke 9:18-20).

What did Peter have in mind with this answer?
Doubless the same thing that the Pharisees had in mind
with their questions--the physical kingdom promises to
Israel. At least two of the other disciples, James and
John, had this conception also when they requested of
Jesus that they might "sit in Your glory, one on Your
right, and one on Your left" (Mark 10:37). This
glorious Messianic kingdom was the universal anticipation of the Jewish nation. The disciples were no
different.[9] This is why Jesus follows Peter's answer
immediately by warning and instructing them not to tell
anyone of His true identity (Luke 9:21). The kingdom
might be in them spiritually, victory over Satan, sin,
and self was assured by the arrival of the King and
kingdom, but He was "not yet" the glorious King they
anticipated nor was His kingdom the magnificent kingdom
desired that they might be rid of the dreaded Romans.

This universal anticipation and desire can be seen in the cynical yet genuine triumphal entry into Jerusalem (Matthew 21:1-11; Mark 11:1-10; Luke 19:29-38). This is why Jesus follows Peter's confession with the following warning and instruction--the literal kingdom is "not yet":

> "The Son of Man must suffer many things, and be rejected by the elders and chief priests and scribes, and be killed, and be raised up on the third day." And He was saying to them all, "If anyone wishes to come after Me, let him deny himself, and take up his cross daily, and follow Me. For whosoever wishes to save his life shall lose it, but whoever loses his life for my sake, he is the one who will save it. For what is a man profited if he gains the whole world, and loses or forfeits himself?" (Luke 9:22-25).

This was not what Peter had understood by his answer. He and the other disciples were anticipating glory, not martyrdom. The cross for them was not the sign of God's deliverance as it is for us. For them it was parallel to the hangman's noose of nineteenth century America. It was the means of public execution, not glorious victory. It stood for the establishment of Roman rule, not the lifting of the hated yoke by the Christ, God's anointed King of Israel. The cross could not possibly be the desired way. If it was, then there must not be a physical kingdom yet to be fulfilled in Israel. If it was, then not only was Jesus not the Messiah, but such Messianic hope was a false dream, or even worse, a lie perpetuated by the tradition in Israel. The Transfiguration, however, destroys all such doubts and definitively illustrates the theistic splendor of Immanuel, the anointed of God, the King of Israel--the final prophet, priest, and king!

Eight days or so later, the very three that most vocally express their Messianic expectations, Peter, James, and John, are provided absolute proof of Jesus' Messianic identity. For in the midst of prayer, Jesus is metamorphosized (literal Greek) before them. The veil is lifted momentarily. The divine splendor is overwhelming. The gospel writers will later search for adequate analogies to help us comprehend the unique magnificence and infinite glory. Matthew will compare the brilliance of his face with the awesome brightness of the sun (Matthew 17:2). Mark will more mundanely state that His garments were so pure that "no launderer on earth can whiten them" (Mark 9:3). And Luke compares His clothes with the flashing of lightning in a pitch-dark midnight sky (Luke 9:29). But the majestic grandeur is not really the absolute center of the event, though it should substantiate once-and-for all that Jesus is truly the Christ. Rather the primary center of the Transfiguration occurrence is the appearance of Moses and Elijah who speak of the Lord's "exodus" at Jerusalem (Luke 9:30-31). That is, His exodus from life to death, and death to life, because death could not hold Him (Acts 2:24). This was their salvation as well as ours! The historical events of the crucifixion and resurrection bring in the "already" and make secure the "not yet."

But why these two men? Why not Adam the father of the human race and Abraham the father of God's people who were the progenitors of the Messiah? Why is not David, the archtype of the Messiah, appropriate? These questions are answered when we remember the reason for the Transfiguration. It occurs to substantiate that Jesus is the Christ as Peter proclaimed but which Jesus seemed to deny. The Chist is to be the final great prophet (Deuteronomy 18:15, 18), the king (2 Samuel 7:8-13), and the priest, most clearly delineated by hindsight (Psalm 110:4; Hebrews 5:1-10; 7:1-28). Thus Moses, the one through whom God gave the law, sacrificial system, and Levitical priesthood is there to demonstrate that Jesus is the final High Priest since "it is fitting that we should have such a high priest, holy, innocent, undefiled, separated from sinners and exalted above the heavens; who does not need daily, like those high priests [Old Testament priesthood], to offer up sacrifices, first for His own sins, and then for the sins of the people, because this He did once for all when He offered up Himself" (Hebrews 7:26-27). This offering is what Moses and Elijah speak with Him about. Moses' presence indicates that the Old Testament priesthood is being done away with by the Messianic High Priest. The tear in the veil of the curtain before the Holy of Holies at the time of Jesus' death is the absolute demonstration of His priestly accomplishment and Messianic identity (Matthew 27:50, 51).

So too is Jesus the final Prophet (Hebrews 1:1, 2). Elijah as the first great prophet is present to indicate that this is the One to Whom all of the prophets looked to and proclaimed. There is no additional revelation. John the Baptist, in prison, receives the answer to his question as to whether Jesus is "the Expected One, or shall we look for someone else?" (Matthew 11:2, 3) by Jesus pointing to the empirical evidence of His miracles that were uniquely the power and work of the anticipated Messiah (Matthew 11:4-6).

The Final Priest, the Final Prophet, the Promised King, and yet Peter misunderstands the entire significance of the Transfiguration because of his sleepiness. Rather than seeing Jesus as the Ultimate, the Messianic completion of the work and ministry of Moses and Elijah, he implies their equality by suggesting three monuments to commemorate the event. Luke correctly editorializes by writing that Peter was "not realizing what he was saying" (Luke (9:33). The climax then occurs for "a voice came out of the cloud, saying, 'This is My Son, My Chosen One; listen to Him!'" (Luke 9:35). Special revelation is both complete and final in the Person of the enfleshed God-man.

The Transfiguration demonstrates that the kingdom of God is more than figurative or spiritual. While the kingdom of God is most definitely the rule of God in our hearts made possible by means of a peace with God through the finished work of the Messianic High Priest (Romans 5:9; Colossians 3:15), it will also have a divine splendor to match the splendor of the King, God's Son, as revealed at the Transfiguration. The kingdom of God is "already" in our midst, it is literally "in us" as regenerated new creations (2 Corinthians 5:17). But there is a "not yet" as well as an "already" dimension of the New Covenant. Hebrews 8:7-12, quoting Jeremiah 31:31-34, implies both an "already" and a "not yet." It reads thusly:

> For if that first covenant had
>   been faultless,
> There would have been no occasion
>   sought for a second. For
>   finding fault with them, He
>   says,
> "Behold, days are coming, says the
>   LORD,
> When I will effect a new covenant

170

With the house of Israel and with
the house of Judah;
Not like the covenant which I made
with their fathers
On the day when I took them by the
hand
To lead them out of the land of
Egypt;
For they did not continue in My
covenant,
And I did not care for them, says
the LORD.
For this is the covenant that I
will make with the house of
Israel
After those days, says the LORD:
I will put My laws into their
minds,
And I will write upon their hearts.
And I will be their God,
And they shall be My people.
And they shall not teach everyone
his fellow citizen,
And everyone his brother, saying
'Know the LORD,'
For all shall know Me,
From the least to the greatest of
them.
For I will be merciful to their
iniquities,
And I will remember their sins no
more."

Most certainly the New Covenant has to do with the
Jews. It was originally stated by God for Israel and
Judah through Jeremiah just prior to the utter destruction of Jerusalem by Nebuchadnezzar and the beginning
of the Babylonian captivity for Judah. Israel, the ten
northern tribes, had already been carried away by
Assyria nearly 140 years earlier. But this is God's
promise, His guarantee, that neither Israel nor Judah
will be forgotten. Both will return to their God!
(See also Isaiah 11:11, 12 and Ezekiel 37:15-28.) It
will be a relationship that not only will be universal
within Israel, but perpetual. It will not be broken by
sin and Jewish waywardness as the Mosaic covenant,
necessitating judgmental captivity. The reiteration of
the New Covenant in the book of Hebrews most certainly
implies that this is still God's commitment to physical

Israel. How could it be taken in any other way by first-century Jewish readers of this epistle?

We have seen that Jesus definitely teaches that the kingdom of God is "already." But this does not mean that there is no future and physical promise to be fulfilled for the nation of Israel. In Matthew 19:28 Jesus assuredly visualizes the future and physical reality of the kingdom blessings to Israel every bit as much as He knows the kingdom of God is also presently within us:

> And Jesus said to them [disciples],
> "Truly I say to you, that you who
> have followed Me, in the regenera-
> tion when the Son of Man will sit
> on His glorious throne, you also
> shall sit upon twelve thrones,
> judging the twelve tribes of
> Israel."

It is impossible to make this very specific reference to the "twelve tribes" apply to the Church (see also Luke 22:28-30). It is Christ's clear proclamation of the future for Israel in "the regeneration," a future when all is "born-anew." Regeneration is the same word in the Greek text that usually refers to the new creation from death to life as children of God, the second birth. A period, then, that Christ identifies as "the regeneration" must be the time that Isaiah 11 pictures when "the wolf will dwell with the lamb, and the leopard will lie down with the kid" and "the earth will be full of the knowledge of the LORD as the waters cover the sea" (Isaiah 11:6, 9). This latter aspect is identical with the promise of the New Covenant that "all shall know Me, from the least to the greatest of them" (Jeremiah 31:34; Hebrews 8:11). Hebrews, following Christ, knows that the "not yet" of the kingdom is future.

This hope for the future kingdom permeated the minds of the disciples also, both in the despair of the crucifixion and the joy of the resurrection. In Luke 24:21 the now hopeless disciples mutter "we were hoping that it was He who was going to redeem Israel." They understood Christ's promise of Matthew 19:28 perhaps too well! "How can Israel be redeemed, repurchased, and sets free for 'the regeneration,' if the man Jesus of Nazareth, who we took to be the Christ, is now dead?" Jesus, of course, had prompted this question as

a shrouded and undisclosed fellow-traveler. He would
soon give an exhaustive exposition of the Scriptures
"from Moses and from all the prophets" concerning the
person and work of the Christ (Luke 24:27). In no way
are we led to believe that the disciples are wrong to
be expecting a literal kingdom on earth for Israel.
Very similar treatment is given the disciples' question
just prior to the Ascension, "Lord, is it at this time
You are restoring the kingdom to Israel?" (Acts 1:6).
The question probably was prompted by what Luke tells
us of Christ's "speaking of the things concerning the
kingdom of God" during the preceding days (Acts 1:3).
In any case, they are certainly not rebuked for such
conceptions, but actually confirmed, by the Lord's
reply that "it is not for you to know times or epochs
which the Father has fixed by His own authority" (Acts
1:7). The literal kingdom of God is affirmed as a yet
future epoch. The Greek word is _kairos_ which is a
definite point of time with a fixed content (note Luke
19:44; 21:8; 1 Thessalonians 5:1; 1 Timothy 5:14, 15;
1 Peter 1:5, 11; Revelation 1:3; 11:18). The line
concerning the various epochs (_kairoi_) still has a way
to go. History is always moving onwards with direction
and purpose under the divine sovereignty and providence. There is at least one historical _kairoi_ left!
The kingdom of God in and for Israel is "not yet."

This does not mean there is no present-day
application, or even fulfillment, of the New Covenant.
Peter saw that the outpouring of the Holy Spirit,
promised by Joel for the last time, was "already." The
context of the Joel prophecy most definitely refers to
Israel. Joel 2:27, prior to the prediction of the
pouring out of the Holy Spirit in verse 28, says that
"you will know that I am in the midst of Israel, and
that I am the LORD your God, and there is no other; and
My people will never be put to shame." This, of
course, must refer to the incarnation, unless Peter
made a mistake in interpretation, for Joel 2:28 reads
that "it will come about _after_ _this_, that I will pour
out My Spirit on _all_ _mankind_" (i.e. Jews and Gentiles)
[italics added]. That is what happened at Cornelius'
Gentile home, prompting Peter to reply to the Jews who
"were amazed because the gift of the Holy Spirit had
been poured upon the Gentiles also" that "surely no one
can refuse the water for those to be baptized who have
received the Holy Spirit just as we did, can he?" (Acts
10:45, 47). Peter had hinted of this development,
probably because of Joel's statement, when he concluded
his Pentecost sermon that the Jews were to repent,

173

receive forgiveness, and "receive the gift of the Holy
Spirit, for the promise is for you and your children,
and for those who are afar off" (Acts 2:38, 39)
[italics added]. The primary aspect for us to note is
that the pouring out of the Spirit was exclusively on
Jews at Pentecost. This is the "pledge" to the Jewish
people that the literal manifestations of God's kingdom
will "yet be" even if it is "not yet." The gift of the
Holy Spirit is the "pledge" of the New Covenant that "I
will be their God and they shall be My people." The
Jews have the "already" of the New Covenant in the
kingdom of God that is "in your midst" even as all
mankind. It is the "already" of the "new life" which
is the first fruit pointing toward the physical and
tangible "redemption of our body" (Romans 8:23; see
also 1 Corinthians 15:20-24). This real but spiritual
manifestation will yet be tangible and physical in both
the resurrection of our bodies and the establishment of
the kingdom. Jesus implies this at the Last Supper in
His allusion to the New Covenant when he says "this is
My blood of the covenant, which is poured out for many.
Truly I say to you, I shall never again drink of the
fruit of the vine until the day when I drink it new in
the kingdom of God" (Mark 14:24, 25; see also Matthew
26:27-29; Luke 22:17, 18). There seems to be no
reason, given Christ's continued promise of a kingdom
to Israel even after announcing that the kingdom of God
was in our midst (Matthew 12:28; 19:28; Luke 17:20, 21;
Zechariah 13:7-14:9), that all this is not synonymous
with the literal and historical Millennium of Revelation 20:1-4 that begins at Christ's Second Coming.
Then what Paul terms a "partial hardening" of Israel
will cease and "all Israel will be saved." Paul
intuitively connects this with the promise of the
Messiah and the New Covenant by referring to Isaiah
59:21 and Jeremiah 31:33, 34 as authoritative Scriptural support for Israel's yet future salvation:

> All Israel will be saved: just as
>   it is written,
> "The Deliverer will come from Zion,
> He will remove ungodliness from
>   Jacob.
> And this is My covenant with them,
> When I take away their sins"
>   (Romans 11:26, 27).

Last things is thus not different in kind from all
the rest of the doctrines we have examined. Like them,
there are two facets that must be equally emphasized.

We have found no biblical reason to maintain that the kingdom of God is only future, nor that the kingdom promises are fulfilled totally but figuratively in the present rule of God in the heart of regenerated believers. Like the Person of Christ, or the inspiration of Scripture, two sides or facts must be maintained simultaneously to be biblical. In other words, the kingdom of God is <u>both</u> "already" <u>and</u> "not yet." This does not answer all the questions nor settle all the issues of the doctrine of last things. But it is an essential and indispensable starting point that also demonstrates the balance and even-handed possibilities instead of the many exclusive, but erroneous, positions we too hastily adopt.

REFLECTION

1. List the primary points of difference among conservative Christians within the doctrine of last things. Briefly state how the "already and the not yet" attempts to unify these differences.

2. Identify the "last days" from an Old Testament perspective. Substantiate this understanding from various New Testament perspectives.

3. What was the essence of the Messianic hope in first century Judaism? Provide evidence that the Apostles shared this hope. Why might the disciples misunderstand the words and actions of Jesus when these are interpreted from this orientation?

4. How does the Transfiguration aid in dispelling these misunderstandings and doubts of the disciples? What is the center of the conversation of the two guest participants at the Transfiguration? Why is this so important to these two Old Testament saints? (Note Romans 3:25, 26.) Why are these two the representatives of the Old Testament?

5. Discuss the New Covenant in the context of the Last Supper (Matthew 26:26-29; Mark 14:22-25; Luke 22:17-20) and the book of Hebrews 8:7-12. Is there any possible debate that the New Covenant is other than "already and not yet"? Relate the provision of the Holy Spirit to the New Covenant and the implications for the doctrine of last things.

6. What post-resurrection indications are there that the disciple were still expecting a literal kingdom? Were they reproved for such by Jesus? Did He in any way encourage these beliefs and expectations?

7. Review each of the twelve doctrines presented in this book. Is biblical balance necessary? Why? Have theological liberals and conservatives often been found at unbiblical extremes? Is this also true of many of the theological debates within evangelical circles?

ENDNOTES

[1]L. Berkhof, Systematic Theology (Grand Rapids: William B. Eerdmans Publishing Company, 1939), pp. 406-411, 708-711.

[2]Emery H. Bancroft, Christian Theology, edited and revised by Ronald B. Mayers (Grand Rapids: Zondervan Publishing House, 1976), pp. 284-288, 358-365.

[3]Oscar Cullmann, Christ and Time, revised edition; translated by Floyd V. Filson (Philadelphia: Westminster Press, 1964).

[4]This did not become a universal practice in Christendom until the eighteenth century. In the medieval era and later it was customary to date as Judaism from creation, though many spoke of the "years of the Lord" for the years following Christ's birth.

[5]Cullmann, op. cit., p. 19.

[6]F. E. Marsh, Emblems of the Holy Spirit (Grand Rapids: Kregel Publications, 1957), p. 256.

[7]Cullmann, op. cit., p. 72.

[8]R. C. H. Lenski, The Interpretation of The Epistles of St. Peter, St. John and St. Jude (Minneapolis: Augsburg Publishing Company, 1961), pp. 430-431.

[9]Simon, the Zealot, was most certainly attracted to Jesus by the hope that Christ might be the One to "redeem Israel" (Luke 24:21). Some New Testament scholars also contend that Judas' human motivation was to put Jesus in such a compromising position He would finally assert His true power if threatened by the Roman authorities. See, for instance, Oscar Cullmann, The State in the New Testament (New York: Charles Scribner's Sons, 1956), pp. 8-23.

CHAPTER XIV

EVANGELICAL PERSPECTIVES: TOWARD A BIBLICAL BALANCE

The preceding pages have attempted to provide a resting place for many of the doctrinal differences within evangelical Protestantism. Obviously, all will not feel called to rest in these places. It is the contention here, however, that the balance that the Bible declares on these doctrinal areas is not found at the limits of the spectrum in regard to these various issues. This is clear if one simply considers the first three doctrines discussed.

Certainly, orthodox Christianity has never identified God with creation, nor has it denied the deity of Jesus Christ while affirming His complete humanity. The latter being the case, the doctrine of the Trinity has been and is the ground floor of Christian theology. These three theological doctrines are all unanimously accepted across evangelical Protestantism, yea across all of Christendom including Roman Catholicism and Eastern Orthodoxy. But this was not always the case. Neo-platonic influences in the early church attempted to interpret creation as emanation and thus God and everything else were ultimately identical. Similarly, the attempt to delineate a biblical outlook in regard to Jesus Christ from the data of the text was difficult to say the least. Nevertheless, one could not claim he was merely a man like other men. Human he most definitely was. He had come forth from the womb like every other man. He slept, ate, thirsted, etc.; he even was tempted to sin. But he was definitely more than man. Not only were his public and private claims extraordinary, but his knowledge, actions, prayer-life, demeanor, and lastly, his resurrection demonstrated the truth of his claims. There were no options to understand his Person other than that of balance. The Bible presented him as both divine and human. The controversy over the Godhead was merely an extension of the controversy over the Person of Jesus. Once it was determined that biblical teaching left no alternative but that he was the unique Son of God, the incarnated deity, the one the Old Testament prophet Isaiah named Immanuel, then the doctrine of the trinity was theologically constructed from the irrefutable data of the biblical material for both Jesus, the Christ, and the Holy Spirit who took his place.

179

It is this balance evidenced in the theological debates of the early church that we need to model in the contemporary church. The conservative Christian world is not only divided over the nature of Scripture in a manner similar to the debates over the divine/human nature of Jesus. We also cannot agree on the nature of man as we dance between a pessimistic view of man that borders on the meaninglessness of existentialism's man, or flirt with a Christian humanism that occasionally seems to apotheosize man very similarly to the secularist whom we all claim to dread. A movement toward a biblical balance that declares Scripture to be God's through the instrumentality of man in his historical and cultural contexts is needed. But so also is an anthropology that recognizes man's worth both ontologically and soteriologically while not overlooking his penchant to lose the purview of his intrinsic value via an independent drift to meaninglessness. At least a movement toward a biblical balance is what has been sketched above in regard to both man himself and man's involvement and inspiration in the penning of the Bible. Hopefully, this work is only a first step, certainly not a last step, in achieving the biblical balance that all evangelicals desire in their doctrinal expositions and systematic theologies.

When speaking of the Bible as the uniquely inspired Word of God, we must remember that inspiration is not the fundamental truth. Rather the Bible is inspired <u>because</u> it is the record of God's special and historical uncovering of Himself for man's knowledge and redemptive benefit. Therefore, the primary aspect of revelation is not the written word, but the event that the written word preserves for us. For instance, it is not the words of Matthew 27 and 28 that record the crucifixion and resurrection that are the redemptive means, but the first century events that enable us to be redeemed. This does not mean, as noted in chapter 7, that the Bible is then of no real significance. The <u>Bible</u> is <u>revelation</u> as it provides us a record of those climactic events of the life of Christ (Hebrews 1:1-8) as well as the Old Testament history that was also revelatory of God's nature through God's dealings with Adam, Noah, Abraham, Isaac, Jacob, Joseph, Moses, Joshua, David, etc., or with the nation of Israel as a whole in provision or judgment. The Bible as God's Word is not magical nor mystical. It is unique, yes; but it is to be read and understood as any other piece of great literature. Its uniqueness is in its divine content and message as well as its origin. But it in itself is not to be worshipped. Rather it is the means of knowing God and therefore accepting His message on His terms. Both Testaments are God-given for our benefit as Paul reminds us in regard to the Old Testament in his Corinthian epistle: "These things happened to them as examples and were written down as warning for us, on whom the fulfillment of the ages has come" (1 Corinthians 10:11; see also vss. 1-10). The Old Testament expectation had been fulfilled in Jesus as the Christ, the Messiah, but the Old Testament is still every bit God's uniquely inspired recorded word of his historical doings for the edification and instruction of His beloved people throughout all ages.

General, or natural, revelation is, like special revelation, two-fold. By this we mean that general revelation is not seen simply in the grandeur of starry nights, waterfalls, or mountain sunsets, nor in the physics laboratory, astronomy telescope, or high-powered microscope of cellular biology. Certainly, it is seen there "for since the creation of the world God's invisible qualities--his eternal power and divine nature--have been clearly seen, being understood from what has been made . . ." (Romans 1:20). So-called creation science is not the only expression, nor the most important one, of general revelation, however. For it, unlike the second expression built within man's psyche, may be intellectually dismissed through philosophy or evolutionary science. Thus Paul also writes that "what may be known about God is plain to them, because God has made it plain to them," or perhaps better, "in them" (Romans 1:19). The witness of God's reality is always with man for man cannot escape himself. A biblically balanced anthropology is thus epistemologically significant. Man made in God's image cannot forget God without forsaking his own ontology. This being impossible, it is then impossible for man totally to eradicate an intuitive knowledge of God from his life apart from suicide. General revelation, then, speaks effortlessly, but effectively and eloquently if wordlessly, of God's glory and eternal presence.

> The heavens declare the glory of
>   God;
> the skies proclaim the work of his
>   hand.
> Day after day they pour forth
>   speech;

night after night they display
knowledge.
There is no speech or language
where their voice is not heard.
Their voice goes out into all the
earth,
their words to the ends of the
world
(Psalm 19:1-4, NIV).

There is another division within conservative
Protestantism, that while it may not be completely
healed, does seem to be mending. That is the issue of
the relationship between the testaments. Here certainly balance is needed. While they obviously are not
identical in message and purpose, or there would be no
need of two, at the same time the division of the two
cannot be so pronounced as to practically excise the
Old Testament from the Christian Bible. As noted in
chapter 9, only a theology that proclaims <u>both</u> continuity <u>and</u> discontinuity is truly balanced biblically.
The reference of Paul noting the purpose and significance of Old Testament history to Corinthian Christians
points to the continuity between the two eras. The
entire book of Hebrews is written for this very
purpose. There is both promise and fulfillment and the
continuity between the testaments is most clearly seen
in this theological context. Such promise and fulfillment does not remove all facets of discontinuity,
however. Most certainly there is a difference in the
called-out church and the called-out nation. What was
appropriate for the old nation is not necessarily
appropriate for the new church. How to absolutely
delineate these differences, or discontinuity, is not
always easy. Paul's epistle to the Galatians and his
reference to the nation in Romans 9-11 demonstrate that
Paul realized there was discontinuity every bit as much
as he evidenced continuity in so many passages. This
Pauline balance of continuity/discontinuity must be
recaptured in the contemporary church. If it is, there
will doubtless be a greater balance also demonstrated
in the doctrines of the church and her future destina-
tion.

Before summarizing the needed balance in regard to
the church and last things, let us turn our attention
to perhaps the widest theological chasm within evangelicalism, the chasm of God's grace and man's free will
in regard to either the inception or continuation of
one's salvation. Nearly everyone gives lip-service to

182

these doctrinal propositions, but little balance is usually achieved. Reformed theologians often so stress God's initiative that there is very little, if any room, for man's response. Wesleyan systematics frequently put so much emphasis on man that the sovereignty of God is overly attenuated if not denied. These teachings, of either tradition, are greatly influenced by their respective anthropologies in which a truly evangelical balance of dignity and depravity is seemingly sacrificed for only one pole of the Bible's teaching. Man is not so depraved that he is incapable of response to God's gracious conviction of sin, righteousness, and judgment (John 16:8-11), nor so independent that he can lose or turn his back upon what God has given in regeneration and the gift of the Holy Spirit. It is the extremes of anthropology that force one theologian to deny at least a response of belief under the prodding of the divine Word and Spirit while another theologian, equally fervent and spiritual, teaches that man can even undo the saving work of God if one wishes. Certainly, man is depraved, but that does not deny his still being in the divine image. Likewise, man having the dignity of the divine image does not make him the equal of God either prior or subsequent to salvation. A balance is needed. Even slight movement by both theologians toward such a balance would provoke a more evangelical perspective to the heart of evangelicalism--the proclamation of the gospel and the saving of souls. Man must be dignified through the divine image or the eternal Son of God could not have been incarnated. But at the same time man must be depraved or there would have been no need of the incarnation. Both traditions would agree that this is the case. Now their soteriologies must be so defined that man's dignity/depravity is remembered in paying heed to the gospel and in the ever-growing walk of holiness of one that is a new creation and thus regenerately secure.

The debate in regard to the primary ministry of the church is not along so well-defined lines as the debate between Reformed and Wesleyan theologies. Here the debate is more one of attitude or outlook. Is the church of Jesus Christ to be eternally focused, or temporally concerned? Why the question is worded in such a mutually exclusive fashion is really a product of the church's experience in American history. Certainly no one would have put the question so glaringly before 1900. The American church had not only been involved with the Revolutionary War and the call for independence, but was temporally involved with the Underground Railroad for runaway slaves as well as becoming more adamant for the abolition of slavery throughout the middle of the century. Similarly, the temperance movement in the last decades of the 19th century was led by the evangelical church as a social and ecclesiastical movement. We have noted in chapter 12 how the so-called social gospel carried this to an extreme in the first decades as it almost completely set aside the eternal ministry of the church. This reverberated in others making the church's ministry only eternal, the salvation of souls. This issue, like the debate over the relationship between the testaments, may be recapturing a biblical balance, a truly evangelical perspective. Let us pray that this is the case. But such prayer must never lead us to forget that the Church, both universally and locally, must always address the ultimate and eternal needs of man. We see this in the ministry of the church throughout the book of Acts, beginning when 3,000 souls accept the initial proclamation of the gospel. We also see the caring by the early church of the temporal needs of her members immediately following the Pentecost address and continuing as seven men, deacons, are appointed to these tasks by the apostles themselves. Such balance is truly an evangelical perspective.

The final doctrinal balance is needed in the final doctrine--the doctrine of last things. This doctrine is integrally related to nearly every other teaching of the Christian church. Christology, anthropology, soteriology, ecclesiology, to name only the most prominent, directly or indirectly determine one's theology in regard to the eschaton. Will Christ rule as a King on this earth? Or is he ruling as a King now in the Church? Are all Old Testament promises to the nation of Israel fulfilled in the church, or are they still to be literally fulfilled in a final manifestation of earthly as well as a heavenly salvation? If Christ rules as King in the Church now, and the national promises of the Old Testament are fulfilled spiritually in the Church, then there is little left for an earthly eschaton. We have discussed these issues in the previous chapter and do not have to reiterate them in summary. Surely, there is a balance that is biblical that is available to theologians of each persuasion. The balance will not eliminate all the questions nor all the divisions. But it will emphasize what the Bible seems to emphasize, that the last days have begun but they are not completed. It is

184

truly an "already" but also a "not yet." Perhaps more detail is not really necessary. We are to live as new creations NOW. We do this by "occupying" UNTIL I COME. Peter tells the Pentecost crowd that the "already" is here for the giving of the Holy Spirit is that which was promised by the prophet Joel and is now being fulfilled (Acts 2:16). Similarly, John writes his beloved children that the "already" has begun because "many antichrists have come" and "this is how we know it is the last hour" (1 John 2:18). A few verses later, John also writes that we are to "continue in him, so that when he appears we may be confident and unashamed before him at his coming" (1 John 2:28; see also 1 John 3:2). There is a "not yet." We have explained such above and need not repeat ourselves in closing. But biblical balance is every bit as essential here as elsewhere if a true evangelical perspective is to be offered to believers and unbelievers alike who are frequently "turned off" by the multiplicity of disagreements by those who claim to know God.

Theologians are never omniscient. Thus no one book can ever provide an absolute stance on these doctrines or issues. This work is intended to provoke a temperate mind-set that encourages us to view these issues from the perspective of both sides. If we would more intensively practice such, then we would be much more hesitant to call our fellow believer and colleague who also desires an all encompassing biblicism and a solid theological orthodoxy either a "heretic" or a "humanist." The contention of this book is that these laudatory goals of biblicism and doctrinal orthodoxy can only be achieved by implementing and practicing the theological equilibrium that the Bible so graciously and consistently proclaims. Therefore to see the entire picture of biblical balance we must move closer to the biblical picture, remove our traditional glasses of whatever hue that frequently warps the picture, and truly desire an evangelical perspective that is biblical. Such perspective need not always escape us, even if we will not exhaustively see it nor express it. We can be moving, not to ever more differentiated theological camps, but toward a biblical balance, an evangelical perspective.

BIBLIOGRAPHY

This bibliography is primarily the totality of all of the books referred to in the text. Therefore a number of the books are Christian classics (Augustine, Calvin, etc.) and many are scholarly and/or reference books. A few books are noted for their historical influence (Gladden, Rauschenbusch, etc.) and others are noted for their helpfulness while being written in a popular style.

A. BOOKS

Albright, William Foxwell. _From the Stone Age to Christianity_. Second edition. New York: Doubleday Anchor Books, 1957.

Augustine. _The Confessions_. Translated by J. G. Pilkington. New York: Liveright Publishing Company, 1943.

_____. _On Free Choice of the Will_. Translated by Anna S. Benjamin and L. H. Hackstaff. Indianapolis: Bobbs-Merrill, 1964.

_____. _On The Predestination of the Saints_ in _Basic Writings of St. Augustine_. Edited by Whitney Oates. Two volumes. Grand Rapids: Baker Book House, 1980.

Baker, David L. _Two Testaments: One Bible_. Downer's Grove, Illinois: Inter-Varsity Press, 1977.

Bancroft, Emery. _Christian Theology_. Edited and revised by Ronald B. Mayers. Grand Rapids: Zondervan Publishing House, 1976.

Berkhof, L. _Principles of Biblical Interpretation_. Grand Rapids: Baker Book House, 1950.

_____. _Systematic Theology_. Grand Rapids: William B. Eerdmans Publishing Company, 1941.

Bickersteth, Edward Henry. _The Holy Spirit_. Grand Rapids: Kregel Publications, 1959.

_____. _The Trinity_. Grand Rapids: Kregel Publications, 1957.

Bruce, A. B. *The Humiliation of Christ*. New York: Hodder and Stoughton, n.d.

Brunner, Emil. *Truth as Encounter*. Translated by Amandus W. Loos, David Cairns, and T. H. L. Parker. Philadelphia: Westminster Press, 1964.

Buber, Martin. *I and Thou*. Translated by Walter Kaufman. New York: Charles Scribner's Sons, 1970.

Calvin, John. *Calvin Commentaries*. Eight volumes. Grand Rapids: A & P Publishers, n.d.

_____. *Institutes of the Christian Religion*. Translated by Henry Beveridge. Grand Rapids: William B. Eerdmans Publishing Company, 1964.

Carey, George. *I Believe in Man*. Grand Rapids: Eerdmans Publishing Company, 1977.

Chafer, Lewis Sperry. *Systematic Theology*. Eight volumes. Dallas: Dallas Seminary Press, 1964.

Clouse, Robert G. *The Meaning of the Millennium*. Downers Grove, Illinois: Inter-Varsity Press, 1977.

Corduan, Winfried. *Handmaid to Theology*. Grand Rapids: Baker Book House, 1981.

Cullmann, Oscar. *Christ and Time*. Revised edition. Translated by Floyd V. Filson. Philadelphia: Westminster Press, 1964.

_____. *The State in the New Testament*. New York: Charles Scribner's Sons, 1956.

Davis, John Jefferson (editor). *The Necessity of Theology*. Second edition. Grand Rapids: Baker Book House, 1978.

Filler, Louis. *The Crusade Against Slavery*. New York: Harper Torchbooks, 1960.

Geisler, Norman L. *Inerrancy*. Grand Rapids: Zondervan Publishing Company, 1979.

_____. Biblical Errancy: An Analysis of Its Philosophical Roots. Grand Rapids: Zondervan Publishing House, 1981.

Gladden, Washington. The Church and Modern Life. Boston: Houghton Mifflin, 1908.

Godet, Frederick. Commentary on the Gospel of John. Two volumes. Translated by Timothy Dwight. Grand Rapids: Zondervan Publishing House, n.d.

_____. Commentary on the Epistle to the Romans. Translated by A. Cusin. Grand Rapids: Zondervan Publishing House, 1956.

Kaiser, Walter C. Toward an Old Testament Theology. Grand Rapids: Zondervan Publishing House, 1978.

Kantzer, Kenneth (editor). Evangelical Roots. Nashville: Thomas Nelson, 1978.

Kelly, J. N. D. Early Christian Doctrines. Second edition. New York: Harper & Row, 1960.

Kline, Meredith G. Images of the Spirit. Grand Rapids: Baker Book House, 1980.

Ladd, George Eldon. The New Testament and Criticism. Grand Rapids: William B. Eerdmans Publishing Company, 1967.

_____. The Last Things. Grand Rapids: William B. Eerdmans Publishing Company, 1977.

Lake, Kirsopp. The Religion of Yesterday and Tomorrow. Boston: Houghton Mifflin, 1926.

Leibniz, Gottfried Wilhelm. Discourses on Metaphysics. Translated by George Montgomery. Garden City, New York: Dolphin Books, n.d.

Lenski, R. C. H. The Interpretation of the Epistles of St. Peter, St. John and St. Jude. Minneapolis: Augsburg Publishing House, 1961.

Lewis, C. S. Abolition of Man. New York: Macmillan, 1961.

_____. Mere Christianity. New York: Macmillan, 1943, 1960.

189

Liddell, Henry George and Robert Scott. A Greek-English Lexicon. Ninth edition. Oxford University Pres, 1895.

Marsh, F. E. Emblems of the Holy Spirit. Grand Rapids: Kregel Publications, 1957.

Mayers, Ronald. Both/And: A Balanced Apologetic. Chicago: Moody Press, 1984.

_____. Religious Ministry in a Transcendentless World. Washington, D.C.: University Press of America, 1980.

Montgomery, John Warwick (editor). God's Inerrant Word. Minneapolis: Bethany Fellowship, 1974.

Morgan, G. Campbell. The Crises of the Christ. Westwood, New Jersey: Fleming H. Revell, 1936.

Muller, Jac J. The Epistle of Paul to the Philippians and to Philemon. In The New International Commentary on the New Testament. Edited by Ned B. Stonehouse. Grand Rapids: William B. Eerdmans Publishing Company, 1955.

Packer, J. I. "Fundamentalism" and the Word of God. Grand Rapids: William B. Eerdmans Publishing Company, 1972.

_____. God Has Spoken. Downers Grove, Illinois: Inter-Varsity, 1979.

Pascal, Blaise. The Thoughts of Blaise Pascal. Edited by Brunschvicg. Garden City, New York: Doubleday, n.d.

Pinnock, Clark. Biblical Revelation. Chicago: Moody Press, 1971.

Ramm, Bernard. Protestant Biblical Interpretation. Boston: W. A. Wilde Company, 1956.

_____. Special Revelation and the Word of God. Grand Rapids: William B. Eerdmans Publishing Company, 1961.

Rauschenbusch, Walter. Christianity and the Social Crisis. New York: Macmillan, 1907.

190

        . A Theology of the Social Gospel. New York: Abingdon, 1917.

Richardson, Cyril (editor and translator). Early Christian Fathers. Volume one of The Library of Christian Classics. Philadelphia: Westminster Press, 1953.

Robertson, A. T. Word Pictures in the New Testament. Six volumes. Nashville: Broadman Press, 1932.

Robinson, A. Wheeler. Inspiration and Revelation in the Old Testament. Oxford: Oxford University Press, 1946.

Ryrie, Charles Caldwell. Balancing the Christian Life. Chicago: Moody Press, 1969.

Salmond, S. D. F. The Epistle of Paul to the Ephesians. In The Expositor's Greek New Testament. Edited by W. Robertson Nicoll. Five volumes. Grand Rapids: William B. Eerdmans Publishing Company, 1961.

Sartre, Jean-Paul. Existentialism and Human Emotions. New York: Philosophical Library, 1957.

Schaeffer, Francis. The God Who Is There. Chicago: Inter-Varsity Press, 1968.

        . Death in the City. Downers Grove, Illinois: Inter-Varsity Press, 1969.

        . He Is There and He Is Not Silent. Wheaton, Illinois: Tyndale House Publishers, 1972.

        . How Should We Then Live. Old Tappan, New Jersey: Fleming H. Revell Company, 1976.

        . Christian Manifesto. Westchester, Illinois: Crossway Books, 1981.

Scofield, C. I. Rightly Dividing the Word of Truth. New York: Loizeaux Brothers, 1896.

Smith, Timothy. Revivalism and Social Reform. New York: Harper Torchbooks, 1967.

Sproul, R. C. Knowing Scripture. Downer's Grove, Illinois: Inter-Varsity Press, 1978.

Stibbs, Alan M. *Understanding God's Word.* London: Inter-Varsity Fellowship, 1950.

Strachan, R. H. *The Second Epistle of Peter.* In *The Expositor's Greek New Testament.* Edited by W. Robertson Nicoll. Five volumes. Grand Rapids: William B. Eerdmans Publishing Company, 1961.

Strong, Augustus H. *Systematic Theology.* Three volumes in one. Westwood, New Jersey: Fleming H. Revell Company, 1907, 1962.

Tenney, Merrill C. (editor). *The Bible--the Living Word of Revelation.* Grand Rapids: Zondervan Publishing Company, 1968.

Thiessen, Henry C. *Lectures in Systematic Theology.* Revised by Vernon D. Doerksen. Grand Rapids: William B. Eerdmans Publishing Company, 1979.

Thomas, W. H. Griffith. *St. Paul's Epistle to the Romans.* Grand Rapids: William B. Eerdmans Publishing Company, 1946.

_____. *The Holy Spirit of God.* Grand Rapids: William B. Eerdmans Publishing Company, 1972.

Torrance, Thomas Forsyth. *The Ground and Grammar of Theology.* Charlottesville: University of Virginia Press, 1980.

Trench, Richard Chenevix. *Synonyms of the New Testament.* Grand Rapids: William B. Eerdmans Publishing Company, 1953.

Vincent, Marvin. *Word Studies in the New Testament.* Four volumes. Grand Rapids: William B. Eerdmans Publishing Company, 1946.

Warfield, Benjamin B. *The Inspiration and Authority of the Bible.* Philadelphia: The Presbyterian and Reformed Publishing Company, 1948.

Wells, David F. and John D. Woodbridge (editors). *The Evangelicals.* Nashville: Abingdon, 1975.

Wemp, C. Sumner. *How On Earth Can I Be Spiritual.* Nashville: Thomas Nelson, Inc., 1978.

Wood, Leon. _The Bible and Future Events_. Grand Rapids: Zondervan Publishing House, 1973.

_____. _The Holy Spirit in the Old Testament_. Grand Rapids: Zondervan Publishing House, 1976.

B. ARTICLES

Barker, Kenneth L. "False Dichotomies Between the Testaments," _Journal of the Evangelical Theological Society_, XXV (March, 1982), 3-16.

Frame, John M. "God and Biblical Language: Transcendence and Immanence," _God's Inerrant Word_. Edited by John Warwick Montgomery. Minneapolis: Bethany Fellowship, 1974.

Harris, R. Laird. "The Problem of Communication," _The Bible--the Living Word of Revelation_. Edited by Merrill Tenney. Grand Rapids: Zondervan Publishing House, 1968.

Hughes, Philip Edgcumbe. "Sanctify, Sanctification," _Dictionary of Theology_. Edited by Everett F. Harrison. Grand Rapids: Baker Book House, 1960.